麦格希 中英双语阅读文库

成长的烦恼

第1辑

【美】希伯特 (Ruth Siburt) ●主编

刘慧　匡颖●译

麦格希中英双语阅读文库编委会●编

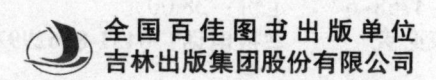

全国百佳图书出版单位
吉林出版集团股份有限公司

图书在版编目（CIP）数据

成长的烦恼. 第1辑 /（美）希伯特（Ruth Siburt）主编；麦格希中英双语阅读文库编委会编；刘慧，匡颖译. -- 2版. -- 长春：吉林出版集团股份有限公司，2018.3（2022.1重印）
（麦格希中英双语阅读文库）
ISBN 978-7-5581-4758-6

Ⅰ.①成… Ⅱ.①希… ②麦… ③刘… ④匡… Ⅲ.①英语—汉语—对照读物②故事—作品集—美国—现代 Ⅳ.①H319.4：I

中国版本图书馆CIP数据核字(2018)第046546号

成长的烦恼　第1辑

编	麦格希中英双语阅读文库编委会
插　画	齐　航　李延霞
责任编辑	欧阳鹏
封面设计	冯冯翼
开　本	660mm×960mm　1/16
字　数	231千字
印　张	10.25
版　次	2018年3月第2版
印　次	2022年1月第2次印刷

出　版	吉林出版集团股份有限公司
发　行	吉林出版集团外语教育有限公司
地　址	长春市福祉大路5788号龙腾国际大厦B座7层
	邮编：130011
电　话	总编办：0431-81629929
	发行部：0431-81629927　0431-81629921(Fax)
印　刷	北京一鑫印务有限责任公司

ISBN 978-7-5581-4758-6　　　定价：38.00元
版权所有　　侵权必究　　举报电话：0431-81629929

前言 *PREFACE*

英国思想家培根说过：阅读使人深刻。阅读的真正目的是获取信息，开拓视野和陶冶情操。从语言学习的角度来说，学习语言若没有大量阅读就如隔靴搔痒，因为阅读中的语言是最丰富、最灵活、最具表现力、最符合生活情景的，同时读物中的情节、故事引人入胜，进而能充分调动读者的阅读兴趣，培养读者的文学修养，至此，语言的学习水到渠成。

"麦格希中英双语阅读文库"在世界范围内选材，涉及科普、社会文化、文学名著、传奇故事、成长励志等多个系列，充分满足英语学习者课外阅读之所需，在阅读中学习英语、提高能力。

◎难度适中

本套图书充分照顾读者的英语学习阶段和水平，从读者的阅读兴趣出发，以难易适中的英语语言为立足点，选材精心、编排合理。

◎精品荟萃

本套图书注重经典阅读与实用阅读并举。既包含国内外脍炙人口、耳熟能详的美文，又包含科普、人文、故事、励志类等多学科的精彩文章。

◎功能实用

本套图书充分体现了双语阅读的功能和优势，充分考虑到读者课外阅读的方便，超出核心词表的词汇均出现在使其意义明显的语境之中，并标注释义。

鉴于编者水平有限，凡不周之处，谬误之处，皆欢迎批评教正。

我们真心地希望本套图书承载的文化知识和英语阅读的策略对提高读者的英语著作欣赏水平和英语运用能力有所裨益。

丛书编委会

Contents

Anna and the Magic Coat
安娜和魔法外衣 / 1

Wonderful Winter
神奇的冬天 / 7

Marcus Loses Patches
马库斯丢了斑斑 / 12

Sparky's Mystery Fortune
斯帕奇的神秘命运 / 19

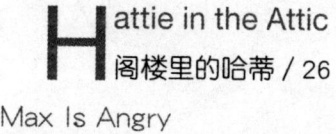

Hattie in the Attic
阁楼里的哈蒂 / 26

Max Is Angry
麦柯斯生气了 / 35

SPRAK!
斯帕拉克! / 44

Eleventeen
11岁 / 59

Becky's Puzzle Problem
贝吉的拼图问题 / 71

Alice's Birthday Cake
爱丽丝的生日蛋糕 / 82

Mirroring Miranda
镜子中的米兰达 / 95

The Mystery Twin
神秘的双胞胎 / 115

Tessa's Family Day
泰莎的家庭日 / 137

Harold the Hungry Plant
哈罗德，饥饿的植物 / 153

01

Anna and the Magic Coat

Anna looked out of her grandmother's window as dark clouds *piled* up in the sky. "I hope it doesn't rain, Oma," Anna said.

"Remember what Opa told you," Oma said. "A little rain makes all things better."

"Not school picnics," said Anna.

"True," Oma nodded, "rain and picnics are not so good."

Anna looked at the box of cupcakes with *pink icing*. Oma and

安娜和魔法外衣

安娜站在奶奶家的窗前向外一望，天上乌云密布。"奶奶，但愿天不下雨，"安娜说。

"记着爷爷跟你说的，"奶奶说，"下点儿雨对所有的东西都有好处。"

"对于学校组织的野餐是不好的，"安娜说。

"当然了，"奶奶点头表示同意，"雨对于野餐没什么好处。"

安娜看着盒子里的纸杯蛋糕，上面还有粉红色的糖霜。安娜和奶奶费

---

pile *v.* 堆放；摞起　　　　　　　　　　　pink *adj.* 粉红色的
icing *n.* 糖霜（用以装饰糕饼）

GROWING PAINS I

Anna had worked hard on them. "Rain is not good for cupcakes, either," said Anna.

Oma tapped her chin. "I wonder if you could..." she *murmured*.

"What?" asked Anna.

"No," Oma said, "you are too young..."

"Tell me!"

"I was thinking," said Oma, "about Opa's *magic* coat."

"Magic coat?" asked Anna.

"It's the long coat, gray as a cloud, that hangs by the door," Oma said.

了好大的力气才做出来这些蛋糕。"下雨对这些纸杯蛋糕来说也不是一件好事，"安娜说。

奶奶轻轻拍着自己的下巴，"我想你是否能……"她小声地说。

"什么？"安娜说。

"不对，"奶奶说，"你还太小……"

"您说吧！"

"我是在想，"奶奶说，"爷爷的魔法外衣。"

"魔法外衣？"安娜问。

"就是那件挂在门边的长大衣，与天上的乌云一样的颜色，"奶奶说。

---

murmur v. 低语　　　　　　　　　　　　　　magic adj. 有魔力的

◆ ANNA AND THE MAGIC COAT

Quickly as *lightning*, Anna ran to get the coat.

"A *sailor* gave it to Opa long ago," said Oma. "Whoever wears it can choose the weather."

Anna put on the coat. "Oof, magic coats are heavy," she said.

She took her cupcakes, ran outside, and shouted at the rain clouds, "Be gone!"

At once, a wind played at Anna's feet. It lifted the bottom of Opa's coat and *spun* up into the sky. The wind *sliced* through the clouds, and the sky turned blue.

"It works!" sang Anna.

安娜像闪电一样，冲到了这件大衣的前面。

"一个海员多年前给你爷爷的，"奶奶说，"无论谁穿上它，都可以选择天气了。"

安娜把这件大衣穿上，"哦，魔法大衣可真的很重，"她说。

她带着她的纸杯蛋糕，跑到了屋外，对着天空的积雨云喊，"请你们离开！"

顿时，她的脚下刮起了大风，吹起爷爷的大衣下摆，风旋转着飘向空中，风把云切成了碎片，天空变得晴朗起来。

"魔法外衣真的有作用了，"安娜唱了起来。

---

lightning *n.* 闪电
spin *v.* （使）快速旋转

sailor *n.* 水手；海员
slice *v.* 切；割

GROWING PAINS I

"Wait!" called Oma, but Anna was too far away to hear.

Anna set her cupcakes on the picnic table.

"*Tag*—you're it!" said Jayda.

Anna tried to run after Jayda, but Opa's coat *wrapped* around her feet.

"You could run better without your coat," Ms. Storm said.

Anna *peeked* at the blue sky. She undid the top button of Opa's coat, and a breeze *tickled* her cheek. She undid the second button, and the breeze blew stronger. She undid the third, and a black cloud

---

"等一下，"奶奶对她喊着，但是安娜离得太远，无法听到奶奶的话。"

安娜把纸杯蛋糕放在野餐桌上。

"捉人游戏——就是你了！"杰达说。

安娜想追上杰达，但是爷爷的大衣裹住了她的双脚。

"你要是把大衣脱下的话，你就能跑得更快。"斯托姆女士说。

安娜透过云彩缝看到蓝色的天空，她解开爷爷大衣的最上面的扣子，微风吹在她的脸上，痒痒的；她解开了第二个扣子，风刮得更大一些了；

---

tag *n.* 捉人（儿童游戏）   wrap *v.* 用……缠绕
peek *v.* 眯着眼睛看   tickle *v.* （使）发痒

went over the sun.

"Oh well, I don't like tag anyway," said Anna. She *buttoned* up the coat, and the sun came back.

"Hide-and-seek!" shouted the children. "Ms. Storm is it!"

Anna hid behind a tree. But Opa's magic coat *stuck out*, and Ms. Storm found her right away.

At last, it was time to eat. But Anna was so hot in the magic coat that her *tummy* hurt. She couldn't eat one bite.

"Darn this magic coat!" Anna said. "What fun is a picnic with no

---

当她解开第三个扣子时，黑色的云彩把太阳遮住了。

"噢，我也不怎么喜欢捉人游戏，"安娜说。她又把大衣的扣子全扣了起来，太阳又出现在天空上。

"捉迷藏！"孩子们喊叫着，"斯托姆女士来找我们！"

安娜躲在一棵树的后面，但是爷爷的魔法大衣露了出来，一下子被斯托姆女士看到了。

最后到了吃饭的时间了，安娜身上的魔法大衣让她热极了，以至于她的肚子也疼起来，她一口东西都吃不下。

"让人讨厌的大衣！"安娜说，"如果没有游戏，也不能吃东西，野

---

button *v.* 用纽扣扣上　　　　　stick out （从某物中）探出；伸出
tummy *n.* 肚子

GROWING PAINS I

games or food?"

Anna undid the buttons of Opa's coat and took it off. The wind *swirled* around her feet and up into the sky. Black clouds piled up, and fat raindrops fell.

"Everyone run into the gym!" shouted Ms. Storm. The children grabbed their plates and ran inside.

Anna hung Opa's magic coat on a *hook*.

"Who wants to play Red Rover?" Jayda asked.

"I do!" said Anna, and she ran, quickly as lightning, to play.

餐一点意思都没有！"

安娜解开了爷爷的大衣，把它脱了下来。风在她的脚下打转，刮向天空。黑云布满了天空，大大的雨点儿落了下来。

"大家快进体育馆，"斯托姆女士大喊着。孩子们抓起自己的餐碟，跑进了体育馆。

安娜把爷爷的魔法大衣挂在一个钩子上。

"谁想玩雷德-雷佛？（儿童分为两组，轮流出一人突破对方手拉手的阵型，如果突不破就成为对方的队员）"，杰达问大家。

"我！"安娜说，接着她就跑去玩了，跑得跟闪电一样快。

---

swirl *v.* （使）打旋；旋动　　　　　　　　　　　　hook *n.* 钩子

02

Wonderful Winter

Elton *hopped* off the school bus, his cheerful yellow *galoshes* going clump-declump, clump-declump. The season's first snow made most kids cheerful. Elton's galoshes were cheerful, but Elton was not. He clump-declumped his way home with an unhappy look on his face.

"Elton, it's snowing," said his mother as he entered the house.

"I know," Elton replied in his *grumpiest* voice. "Tomorrow is Saturday, and there will be nothing to do."

神奇的冬天

埃尔顿蹦跳着下了校车,他的黄色的胶鞋跌跌撞撞。冬天的第一场雪让大多数孩子都非常兴奋。埃尔顿的胶鞋很高兴,但埃尔顿并不是很高兴,他跌跌撞撞地向家里走,满脸不高兴的样子。

"埃尔顿,下雪了,"妈妈看到他进到屋子时说。

"我知道了,"埃尔顿用最生气的语气回答说,"明天是周六,什么事情都做不成。"

---

hop *v.* 跳上(下)　　　　　　　　　　galosh *n.* 橡胶套鞋
grumpy *adj.* 脾气坏的

GROWING PAINS I

Elton loved to be outside during the summer. He loved swimming, hiking, and riding his bike. When the first snow of the winter came, Elton was always sad. He couldn't swim, hike, or ride his bike until spring.

Elton's mother knew he was unhappy. She tried to make him feel better with warm cookies. It only took him a few minutes to eat them all, and then his unhappy face returned.

"Why don't you do your homework?" she *suggested*.

"I finished it at school," he answered.

"Okay, clean your room," she suggested. In fifteen minutes, Elton's room was clean and he was still wearing his unhappy face.

埃尔顿喜欢夏天在户外活动，他喜欢游泳、远足和骑自行车。当冬天的第一场雪来临时，埃尔顿总是非常沮丧。他不能游泳，不能远足，也不能骑自行车了，这些活动都要等到春天。

埃尔顿的妈妈知道他不高兴，就给他一些热乎乎的饼干，希望他能高兴起来。几分钟后他把饼干吃完了，不高兴又回到了他的脸上。

"为什么不做作业呢？"妈妈建议说。

"我在学校里就已经完成了，"他回答说。

"好吧，打扫一下房间吧，"妈妈建议说。15分钟后，埃尔顿的房间就干净了，但他还是不高兴的样子。对于一个喜欢户外的孩子来说，冬

---

suggest *v.* 提议，建议

◆ WONDERFUL WINTER

For an outside boy, winter was a *terrible* time of year.

Just then the doorbell rang—it was Penelope, Elton's friend and next-door neighbor. "Elton, would you like to come outside and make a snowman with me?" Penelope asked. Elton *wrinkled* his nose. He didn't like snow and he didn't like winter.

"Yes, yes, Elton would like to go," his mother said. She *bundled* him up and sent him and his unhappy face outside with Penelope. Penelope and Elton made the largest snowman anyone had never seen. Then they made the tiniest snowman anyone had never seen.

At dinnertime, Elton came inside and his unhappy face was almost gone. But the next morning, it was back again.

天是一年中最糟糕的时间了。

就在这时，门铃响了，是埃尔顿的朋友佩内洛普，也是他们的邻居。"埃尔顿，你想到外面和我一起堆雪人吗？"佩内洛普问。埃尔顿皱起鼻子，他不喜欢雪，他也不喜欢冬天。

"好的，好的。埃尔顿喜欢去，"他妈妈说。妈妈推着他，把他和他的苦脸、佩内洛普一起送到了门外。佩内洛普和埃尔顿一起堆了一个谁都没有见过的最大的雪人，然后又堆了一个谁都没有见过的最小的雪人。

吃晚饭的时候，埃尔顿回到了屋内，脸上的所有不快全部消失，但第二天早上，不高兴的表情又一次出现在脸上。

---

terrible *adj.* 糟糕的
bundle *v.* 匆匆送走；推搡

wrinkle *v.* 皱起

GROWING PAINS 1

"I don't like snow, and I don't like winter," said Elton. Elton's mother *sighed*. Just then the doorbell rang again—it was Penelope.

"Elton, would you like to go *snowshoeing*?" asked Penelope, holding two pairs of snowshoes. Elton wrinkled his nose but said, "Sure, I guess so."

Elton and Penelope *strapped* on the snowshoes and went *stomping* through the trees behind the house.

At lunchtime, Elton came inside without his unhappy face. He

"我不喜欢雪，我不喜欢冬天，"埃尔顿说。埃尔顿的妈妈叹了一口气，这时门铃又响了，是佩内洛普。

"埃尔顿，你想去雪地徒步吗？"佩内洛普问他，她手里拿着两双雪地鞋。埃尔顿皱了一下鼻子，但是说"当然了，我想是的。"

埃尔顿和佩内洛普系好了雪地鞋，迈着重重地步子在房后的树林里走着。

吃午饭的时候，埃尔顿进了屋，脸上没有了不高兴的表情。他告诉妈

---

sigh *v.* 叹气
strap *v.* 系

snowshoe *v.* 穿雪鞋走路
stomp *v.* 迈着重重地步子走

◆ WONDERFUL WINTER

told his mom all about the *adventures* he and Penelope had had in the snow. Just then the doorbell rang—it was Penelope.

"Elton, would you like to go *sledding*?" she said. This time Elton didn't wrinkle his nose. Instead he grabbed his coat and *yelled* to his mom, "I'll be home at dinnertime, with a happy face."

Elton decided that he loved winter. He loved making snowman, going snowshoeing, and sledding. For an outside boy, winter was a *terrific* time of year.

妈他和佩内洛普在雪中所有的历险。这时门铃响了，是佩内洛普。

"埃尔顿，你想玩雪橇吗？"她说。这一次埃尔顿没有皱鼻子，反而是一下子抓起衣服，对妈妈喊了一声，"晚饭时我会高高兴兴回来的。"

埃尔顿决定爱上这个冬天，他喜欢堆雪人，雪地里行走和滑雪橇。对于一个喜欢户外活动的孩子来说，冬天是一年中最好玩的时间。

---

adventure *n.* 历险　　　　　　　　　　　　sled *v.* 乘雪橇
yell *v.* 大声喊　　　　　　　　　　　　　terrific *adj.* 极好的

GROWING PAINS I

03

Marcus Loses Patches

Hi, I'm Marcus, and I love to play video games. So much that my mom thinks I'm *hooked* on them. She might be right. I do spend an *awful* lot of time playing them.

"Marcus, will you feed Patches, please?"

That's my mom, and Patches is my dog. I'm right in the middle of this *awesome* game where I have to find my way through an

---

马库斯丢了斑斑

喂，我是马库斯，我喜欢玩电脑游戏，非常喜欢以至于我妈妈说我已经上瘾了。她这样说可能是对的，因为我在这方面花的时间太多了。

"马库斯你能喂一喂斑斑吗?好不好?"

这就是我妈妈，斑斑是我的狗。我正在玩游戏的关键时刻，我必须找

---

hooked adj. （对某事）着迷　　　　　　awful adj. 很多的，过多的
awesome adj. 让人惊叹的

◆ MARCUS LOSES PATCHES

Egyptian pyramid. I'll get past the sphinx, and then I'll feed Patches.

"Just a minute, Mom."

"All right, but don't forget. I need to get the *casserole* out of the oven for lunch," Mom says.

This game is really difficult. I'll try getting to the *amulet* from the sphinx one more time. Then I'll feed my favorite canine.

Forty-five minutes and several tries later, I hear Mom again.

"Marcus, time to eat."

Perfect timing. Man, is that hardcore—I'm wiped out from dueling the two-headed sphinx to save the magic amulet.

到走出埃及金字塔的路，我得绕过斯芬克斯，然后我再去喂斑斑。

"稍等一下，妈妈。"

"好的，但别忘了，我得把炉子里的砂锅取出来，这是我们的午餐，"妈妈说。

这个游戏太难了，我还得从斯芬克斯那里再取一次护身符，然后再喂我最可爱的狗。

45分钟过去了，我试过好几次了，这时我听到妈妈说话了。

"马库斯，该吃饭了。"

时间刚刚好，哥们，这是最关键的部分——为了拯救魔法护身符，我与双头斯芬克斯决斗时，我被消灭了。

Egyptian *adj.* 埃及的   pyramid *n.* 金字塔
casserole *n.* 砂锅   amulet *n.* 护身符

GROWING PAINS I

I go to the table, and Mom asks if I feed Patches.

Gulp. I'm in big trouble. I got so into my game that I forgot about my dog. I bet Patches is *starving* by now. I know I am.

"Mom, I forgot, I'll feed her now."

I go to the back yard to bring Patches in, but I can't find her. She's not lying under her favorite shade tree. She's not watching our neighbors walk by through the gate.

Wait, the gate's open. Oh no! Patches is gone, lost, nowhere to be found. I must have left the gate *unlatched* when I took her out this morning. I'm in even bigger trouble now.

"Mom, Patches isn't in the yard. I think I might have left the gate

---

我坐到了餐桌前，妈妈问我喂斑斑没有。

我的天呀，我的麻烦大了。我只顾全身心玩游戏了，我把狗给忘了。我想斑斑现在一定是非常饿，连我都是。

"妈妈，我忘了，我得去喂她。"

我来到了院子里，想把斑斑带到屋子里，但她不见了。她没有趴在她最喜欢的树影下，也没有看邻居经过大门。

等一下，大门是开的。噢，不能这样！斑斑逃走了，丢了，不知去哪里了。今天早上我带她出去后，没有拴上大门，现在我的麻烦更大了。

"妈妈，斑斑不在院子里，我想可能是今天早上我没有关好大门，我

---

starve v. （使）挨饿　　　　　　　　unlatch v. 拉开（门等的）插栓

◆ MARCUS LOSES PATCHES

open this morning. I think she escaped."

"She's not there? Marcus, this is bad news," Mom says, "very bad news."

I know she's right, but I'm *torn* between being *psyched* about beating the sphinx and sad about Patches being gone.

I hear Mom making telephone calls trying to *locate* Patches. From what I can hear, it sounds like no one has seen her, and I'm worried. I know what I'll do—I'll make signs so people can contact us if they see Patches. Then I'll go look for her.

Mom helps me make signs even though she's still disappointed in me for being so *irresponsible*. When we finish the signs, we walk

---

猜她是逃跑了。"

"她不在？马库斯，这可不是好消息，"妈妈说，"非常不好的消息。"

我知道妈妈是对的，我正好卡在两件事之间，一面是战胜斯芬克斯的兴奋，另一面是斑斑不见了后的伤心。

我听到妈妈打电话想确定斑斑在哪里，从我听到的内容中可以判断，好像没有人看到这只狗。我有些着急，我知道我该做什么了：我要做一些寻狗启事，因为如果有人看到斑斑他们就可以联系我们，然后我们去找她。

妈妈帮助我做好了寻狗启事，虽然她对我没有责任感很失望。我们做完了寻狗启事后，我们步行在左邻右舍中张贴这些寻狗启事。我们去公

---

torn *adj.* 犹豫的
locate *v.* 确定……的位置

psyched *adj.* 兴奋的；殷切期待的
irresponsible *adj.* 不负责任的

15

GROWING PAINS 1

around the neighborhood to hang them up. We go to the park to see if Patches is there.

My friend Thomas is playing soccer in the park, so I ask Thomas if he's seen Patches. He says he hasn't.

My stomach *growls* loudly as we leave to look elsewhere—I haven't eaten any lunch. Mom asks if I'm okay. I tell her I want to keep looking for Patches. I'm really worried now.

We visit house after house asking neighbors if they have seen Patches. Nobody has.

We're almost to my grandpa's house, a few *blocks* from our place. I'm really hungry. Maybe he'll have a snack—I could use a hug, too. It doesn't seem like we'll ever find Patches.

园，看看斑斑是不是在那里。

我的一个朋友叫托马斯，正在公园里踢足球，我问他是否看到了斑斑，他说没看到。

我的肚子叫声很大，因为我们离家找狗时，没有吃午饭。妈妈问我有没有问题，我告诉她我会继续找斑斑，这回我可真的担心了。

我们挨家挨户地问是不是有人看到了斑斑，可是没有人看到。

我们都快要到爷爷家了，离我们家有几个街区。我真的很饿，可能爷爷会有些零食，我可以给他一个拥抱，看起来我们无法找到斑斑了。

---

growl v. 发出低沉的怒吼　　　　　　　　　　block n. 街区

◆ MARCUS LOSES PATCHES

I knock on Grandpa's door, and I hear *barking*—I hear Patches!

When Grandpa opens the door, Patches jumps up and *licks* my face. I hug her and *pet* her, and even rub her stomach just where she likes.

When we get to grandpa's back yard, Grandpa asks me what happened.

I tell him how I *accidentally* left the back yard gate open and how Patches got out—probably looking for food.

"Can you explain how you forgot to feed her?" Grandpa asks.

"I started playing one of my video games, and I couldn't get past this one part. When I realized Patches was gone, I was so worried."

"How could a video game be more important than your dog?"

我敲了敲爷爷家的门，我听到了狗叫声，这是斑斑的叫声。

爷爷打开门，斑斑一下子跳了起来，用舌头舔我的脸。我把她抱住，拍着她，还搓她的肚子上那块她最喜欢被搓的地方。

我们到了爷爷的后院时，爷爷问我出了什么事情。

我告诉他，我是怎样意外地忘关的后门，斑斑是如何出走的，也许是为了找东西吃。

"你能告诉我你为什么忘了喂她吗？"爷爷问。

"我开始玩电脑游戏，我没能通过那个部分，当然知道斑斑可能走丢时，我也很着急。"

"电脑游戏怎么能比你的狗更重要呢？"爷爷问。

---

bark *v.* （狗）叫　　　　　　lick *v.* 舔
pet *v.* 抚摸　　　　　　　　accidentally *adv.* 意外地

GROWING PAINS I

Grandpa asks.

"It's not," I say.

I'm happy Patches is safe. I feel awful that my dog could have gotten hurt because of me.

I walk over to Mom and Patches.

"Mom, I'm sorry I didn't listen to you, and I'm sorry I made you worry. And Patches, I'm sorry I forgot about you."

"Thank you for the *apology*, Marcus," says Mom. "Let's go home and eat."

I'm sure I'll still forget to do things sometimes. I do love my video games; but I love my mom, my grandpa, and my dog, even more.

"不比狗重要，"我说。

斑斑安全了，我很高兴，我的狗如果因为我的原因受到伤害我会很伤心。

我走到妈妈和斑斑面前。

"妈妈，很对不起没有听你的话，让你如此担心我很抱歉。斑斑，把你忘了，我也很抱歉。"

"感谢你的道歉，马库斯，"妈妈说，"我们一起回家吃饭吧。"

我非常肯定，以后我有时还会忘记事情。我喜欢电脑游戏，但我更爱我的妈妈，我的爷爷，还有我的狗。

---

apology *n.* 道歉

04

Sparky's Mystery Fortune

"Hurry up," said Dad. "Mom is going to wonder where we are. And it's her birthday. We should at least meet her at the restaurant on time."

"Okay, I'll be right there," said seven-year-old Emma.

"Me, too," said Jesse, her elder brother. "Hey, Emma, lock the back gate so the *puppy* can't get out. We'll only be gone an hour or two. It's nice outside. He'll enjoy the fall air and sunshine."

斯帕奇的神秘命运

"抓紧时间,"爸爸说,"妈妈会着急我们到哪里去了。今天是她的生日,至少我们应该及时赶到饭店去见她。"

"好的,没有问题,"七岁的艾玛说。

"我也是,"杰西说,杰西是艾玛的哥哥。"喂,艾玛,把后门锁上,以防小狗出去。我们一两个小时就能回来,外面可真好,它会喜欢秋天的空气和阳光的。"

---

puppy *n.* 小狗

GROWING PAINS I

"Okay," said Emma.

Every year for Mom's birthday, the Mason family *headed* for their favorite Chinese restaurant. It was called the Golden Pagoda. Emma loved the chow mein, and Jesse liked the chop suey. Mom and Dad always ordered egg foo young.

"Just in time," said Mom, as Dad and the children ran *breathlessly* into the restaurant.

In a jiffy, the family was seated, singing Happy Birthday to Mom. She opened her gifts, and everyone ordered their favorite dishes.

"Oh, that was delicious," said Emma. "I'm *stuffed*. But I always have room for a fortune cookie. Besides, it's fun to read the fortune."

"好的，"艾玛说。

每年妈妈的生日，梅森一家都要去中国餐馆的。这个餐馆叫金塔。艾玛喜欢炒面，杰西喜欢炒杂碎，妈妈和爸爸总点芙蓉蛋。

"刚好时间来得及，"妈妈说。爸爸和孩子们气喘吁吁地跑进了饭店。

不一会儿，全家人坐了下来，给妈妈唱生日歌。妈妈打开礼物，每个人都点了最喜欢的饭菜。

"噢，真是好吃，"艾玛说，"我吃得饱饱的了，但我还有地方吃幸运饼干，而且看看自己的运气也很有意思。"

---

head v. 朝……前进　　　　　　　　breathlessly adv. 气喘吁吁地
stuffed adj. 饱的

◆ SPARKY'S MYSTERY FORTUNE

Mom, the birthday girl, opened her cookie first. It read:

You will help solve a mystery.

"Well, how do they know that?" asked Mom, smiling.

Dad opened his cookie next. It read:

What looks like the right road may not be.

"I like to drive," said Dad, laughing.

Jesse opened his fortune cookie next.

You will lose something you care about.

"I hope it's not my *skateboard*," he said.

Then Emma opened up her cookie. The message inside said:

妈妈，就是过生日的人，打开了饼干，上面写着：
你要帮助解开一个秘密。
"嗯，他们怎么知道这事呢？"妈妈笑着问。
接下来爸爸打开了自己的饼干，上面写着：
看起来正确的路，其实不是。
"我喜欢开车，"爸爸大笑着说。
杰西打开自己幸运饼干：
你会失去你最在乎的东西。
"我希望这不是我的滑板，"他说。
最后，艾玛打开了她的饼干，里面的小条写的是：

---

mystery *n.* 秘密   skateboard *n.* 滑板

GROWING PAINS I

Trees keep secrets under their leaves.

"Trees don't have secrets," Emma laughed.

"Let's get one for Sparky so we can find out his fortune," said Jesse.

"Sure," said Dad. "After all, he's a member of our family now."

Jesse asked for another fortune cookie when he asked for a *leftover container*. Jesse mixed the leftovers together while Emma opened Sparky's cookie. It read:

Those around you will be busy while you are at rest.

Huh? thought Emma. "I wonder what that means." Emma *stuffed* all the fortunes in her pocket.

树的叶子下面藏着秘密。

"树是没有秘密的，"艾玛笑了。

"我们给斯帕奇找一个饼干，看看它的运气，"杰西说。

"非常好，"爸爸说，"现在它毕竟是我们家庭的一个成员。"

杰西在要餐盒时，又要了一个运气饼干。杰西得把剩下的饭菜混在一起，艾玛打开斯帕奇的饼干，上面写着：

你自己很清闲，而你周围的人很忙碌。

啊？艾玛想，"我不太明白这是什么意思。"艾玛把所有的运气条放在口袋里。

---

leftover *adj.* 剩余的
stuff *v.* 装满

container *n.* 容器

◆ SPARKY'S MYSTERY FORTUNE

As soon as the family got home, they *discovered* Sparky was missing. Emma had a sick feeling in her stomach.

Emma knew it was her fault. She had forgotten to lock the back gate. The family began to *search* everywhere they thought the puppy might go.

Mom called all of the neighbors. Dad drove around in the family car. Jesse rode his skateboard to the park. But, after an hour, they hadn't found the puppy.

"Where is he?" said Emma, sadly. Then Emma remembered the fortunes in her pocket. She opened the papers and read them again. One fortune caught her *attention*:

全家人回到了家,他们发现斯帕奇不见了,艾玛感到胃很不舒服。

艾玛知道这是她的错误,她忘了锁上后面的大门。全家人到所有小狗可能去的地方去找它。

妈妈给所有的邻居都打过电话,爸爸开着家里的汽车出去找。杰西滑着滑板到公园里找。但是过了一个小时,他们都没有找到小狗。

"它到哪儿去了呢?"艾玛心情沉重地说。这时她想起来口袋里的运气条,打开这些运气条,又读了一遍。有一个运气条引起了她的注意:

---

discover *v.* 发现　　　　　　　　　　　　　　　search *v.* 寻找
attention *n.* 注意力

GROWING PAINS I

Trees keep secrets under their leaves.

"Wait a minute. I think I know where to find him!" Emma shouted. She ran around to the back of the house. Under a pile of leaves *beneath* the *maple* tree, Sparky was curled up, fast asleep.

"There you are," said Emma, as she hugged the puppy. "I guess there are secrets under tree leaves. Well, it doesn't really matter. Finding you is the very best fortune of all!"

Who made the First Fortune Cookie?

We don't know for sure who invented fortune cookies. Here are some *theories*, or guesses.

树的叶子下边藏着秘密。

"等一下，我知道到哪里去找它了！"艾玛大声说。她跑到房子的后面，在那棵枫树下的一堆树叶下面，斯帕奇蜷着身体，熟熟地睡着。

"你在这里呀！"艾玛边抱起小狗边说。"我猜树叶下边有秘密。好的，没有什么。找到你就是最好的运气！"

谁是第一个做运气饼干的人？

我们不能准确说明谁最先发明运气饼干，这里有一些理论或猜想：

---

beneath *prep.* 在……下面 maple *n.* 枫树
theory *n.* 理论

◆ SPARKY'S MYSTERY FORTUNE

Theory 1: Some people think that fortune cookies are modern Chinese moon cakes. Centuries ago, moon cakes with messages inside were common in China.

Theory 2: Makoto Hagiwara invented the cookie around 1910. Hagiwara *founded* Golden Gate Park's Japanese Tea Garden in San Francisco, California. He handed out cookies as thank-you notes.

Theory 3: David Jung invented fortune cookies in Los Angeles in about 1920. Jung founded the Hong Kong Noodle Company. Many people say he handed the cookies out free to *unemployed* men.

However, we do know that today, fortune cookies are enjoyed all over the world.

理论1：有些人认为运气饼干就是现在的中国人吃的月饼。几个世纪前，中国的月饼中有纸条。

理论2：马琴·原在1910年左右发明了运气饼干。马琴·原在加利福尼亚的旧金山建立了金门公园日本茶园，当时他把饼干当成感谢信送给别人。

理论3：大卫·荣于1920年左右在洛杉矶发明了运气饼干，荣建立一家香港面条公司。人们说他给失业的人们发免费的饼干。

不管怎么说，我们知道，运气饼干在全世界都受到欢迎。

---

found *v.* 创办；建立   unemployed *adj.* 失业的

GROWING PAINS I

05

Hattie in the Attic

My name is Hattie MacGruder, and I am special.

At least that's what my Grandma Nettie says. I spent two weeks with her this summer. I didn't want to go, but by the time I got back I was glad I had.

On the last day I was there, I found a hat in my grandma's *attic*. It was a *magical* hat.

I'm not making this up. It really was magical!

阁楼里的哈蒂

我叫哈蒂·麦格鲁德,我与众不同。
至少我的奶奶内蒂是这样说的。今年夏天我与她一起待了两周。开始我不想去,但到了回来的时候,我非常庆幸我去了奶奶家。

在奶奶家的最后一天,我在奶奶的阁楼里发现了一顶帽子,那是一顶魔法帽。

这可不是我瞎编的,这顶帽子真的有魔法。

---

attic *n.* 阁楼   magical *adj.* 有魔法的

◆ HATTIE IN THE ATTIC

When I got back, I told my friends Sybil and Sarah what had happened, but they said I was lying. Well, I am not, and they're liars and *fibbers* and tellers of untruth.

I have *proof* that the hat was magical. The proof is in my diary.

Special Note:

> *I'm not going to let you read that Eric Ledbetter wrote a love note to Sarah. Even though she is a liar and a fibber and a teller of untruth, Sarah would be so **embarrassed** if anyone know Eric had written the love note. Even she doesn't deserve that.*

回到家里后，我告诉我的朋友塞贝尔和莎拉，所发生的一切，但她们说我骗人。我没有骗人，而她们才骗人呢，她们都撒谎，而且她们说的都不是事实。

我有证据表明，这顶帽子有魔法，这些证据就在我的日记之中。

特别注意：

> 我不想让你知道埃里克·莱德贝特给莎拉写过求爱小条。尽管莎拉她骗人，说谎，而且不说实话，但如果有人知道埃里克写过求爱小条的话，她一定不好意思，当然她不应该那样做。

---

fibber *n.* 骗子
embarrassed *adj.* 害羞的

proof *n.* 证据

GROWING PAINS I

Diary, Day 14

Sarah, Sybil, and I had our summer all planned. But Mom, who probably has never had a summer **vacation**, told me tonight that I had to go to Grandma Nettie's home for two weeks.

Two weeks? It might as well be two years. The whole summer will be gone. Sarah and Sybil will be married and have kids by the time I get back.

I don't want to go.

Mom, who probably has never had a summer vacation, just came in and told me to go to sleep. "Big day tomorrow, sweetie!" she **croaked**.

日记，14日

莎拉，塞贝尔和我都计划好暑假了，但妈妈可能没有暑假的经历，所以今晚让我去奶奶内蒂家住两周。

两周?非常有可能是两年的时间。一个暑假就要没了。等我回来时，莎拉和塞贝尔都可能要结婚了，而且都要生了自己的孩子了。

我不想去。

妈妈非常可能没有经历过暑假，走进我的房间，让我睡觉。"明天是一个重要的日子，亲爱的！"她粗声地说。

---

vacation n. 假期   croak v. 用低沉而沙哑的声音说话

◆ HATTIE IN THE ATTIC

Yeah, right! I'll write longer later.

Diary, Day 28 (later . . . a lot later) I am back!

All right, so I forgot my diary. I forgot to pack my **toothbrush**, too!

The two weeks went pretty fast. The last night before I flew home, Grandma Nettie cooked a special dinner, and I set the table. My grandpa died when I was three, but Grandma Nettie always set a place for him.

I don't remember Grandpa very well, but he loved horses and had a horse of his very own. He loved wearing leather **chaps** and his cowboy hat. Grandma said he took me for a ride on his horse once. I kind of remember

---

是呀，好吧！以后我再多写一些吧。

日记28日（不久，很久以后的不久）我回来了！

非常好，所以我忘了写日记了，我还忘了把牙刷带回来了！

两周的时间过得太快了。飞回家的前一天晚上，奶奶内蒂做了一顿特别的晚餐，我摆放桌子。我的爷爷是在我三岁时去世的，但奶奶总要给他留一个位置。

我记不太清爷爷的样子了，但是他喜欢马，而且他自己还有一匹呢。他喜欢穿皮衣服，戴牛仔帽。奶奶说他还曾带我骑过马呢。我有点儿记着这个事，但不是很清楚。

---

toothbrush n. 牙刷   chaps n. 皮套裤

that, but not very well.

After dinner we went into the living room, and both of us read books. Grandma Nettie fell asleep after only two pages of her book.

I must have fallen asleep too, because I woke up with my nose **smashed** on page 34, the very same page where this **brainless** girl is so scared that she pulls the covers over her head, like that's going to save her.

Grandma Nettie was sound asleep in her chair, so I started **prowling** around. Grandma calls this "getting into mischief". I call it prowling around. That's when I went up into the attic.

In all the time that I had been to Grandma's house, I never went up to the attic. I guess that I thought the door was just a closet.

吃完晚饭我们来到起居室，我们都在看书，奶奶内蒂看了两页就睡着了。

我可能也睡着了，因为我醒来时我的鼻子撞在34页上，这页的内容是一个愚蠢的女孩很害怕，所以她把被子蒙在头上，好像这能救她的命一样。

奶奶内蒂在椅子上睡得更香，所以我开始到处溜达，奶奶说我是要"开始做坏事"，而我把这个叫作到处溜达。就在这时，我上了阁楼。

我在奶奶家的所有时间里，从未上过阁楼，我当时认为阁楼的门只不过是一个储藏柜的门。

---

smash v. 猛烈碰撞   brainless adj. 愚蠢的
prowl v. 徘徊

◆ HATTIE IN THE ATTIC

I climbed up the stairs. It was really **spooky**, *just like the book I was reading, but I wasn't scared, not at all. The attic was empty except for an old sweat-stained cowboy hat just lying there in the middle of the floor. I don't know why I did it, but I put on the hat.*

Now this is the hard-to-believe part, but suddenly I wasn't in the attic anymore. I was standing in the middle of a grassy **meadow**. *I heard the* **pounding** *of a horse's* **hooves** *and turned around. Up rode a man on a horse with a red bandanna tied around his neck. His hair was blowing back, and he had a big smile on his face.*

The horse was so beautiful. It was gold colored and had a golden mane

我爬上楼梯,楼梯总是阴森森的,和我读的书一样,但我不害怕,一点都不。阁楼上几乎什么都没有,只有一个很旧的,汗渍很多的牛仔帽放在地板中间。我不知道为什么,我就把它戴在了自己的头上。

现在,这就是让人无法相信的部分,突然,我已经不在阁楼了,我站在一片长满绿草的牧场,我听到马蹄落在地面上的声音,我转过身去。一个人骑着一匹马向我跑来,他的脖子上戴着围巾,他的头发飘向身后,他满脸微笑。

马非常漂亮,它是金黄色的,金黄色的鬃毛、金黄色的尾巴。马在奔跑时头高高地抬起,尾巴在风中摆动着。这个骑马的人径直朝我这里来,勒住马停了下来。马蹄在地上向前滑动,好像还要往前走的样子。马上的

spooky adj. 令人毛骨悚然的
pounding n. 持续的重击声

meadow n. 牧场
hoof n. (马等动物的)蹄

GROWING PAINS I

and tail. It ran with its head up high and its tail snapping in the wind. The man rode right up to me and skidded to a stop. The horse **shuffled** its hooves like it wanted to run some more. The man looked down at me, and as if it were possible, his smile seemed to grow even brighter.

"Hi," he said. "You must be Hattie. You sure have grown."

I didn't say anything. My heart was in my mouth.

The man laughed. Not a **mean** laugh, but a low, happy laugh that made me feel good. "You know," he said, "I sure could use your hat."

With that he reached down and grabbed it. "This will do just fine," he said as he put it on. "Tell you what, I'll trade you."

He pulled the **bandanna** off his neck, reached down, and tied it around my neck. "Isn't much," he said, "but when you wear it, you'll never forget me."

He spun his horse, ready to ride away, but he stopped. Then he reached

---

人向下看着我，好像能看清的样子，他的笑容变得更加明快了。

"嗨，"他说，"你一定是哈蒂吧，你真的是长大了。"

我什么都没有说，我的心都提到嗓子眼儿了。"

这个人笑了，当然不是坏笑，而是一种低沉，但高兴的笑，让我感觉很好。"你知道，"他说，"我想用一下你的帽子。"

这样说着，他伸出手来，抓住了帽子。"非常合适，"他边戴在自己的头上边说，"我们商量一下，我买这顶帽子。"

他从脖子上取下围巾，递给我，系在我的脖子上。"这不算多，"他说，"但是有这个系在脖子上，你就永远不会忘记我的。"

他把马转了一圈，马上就要走了，但他又停了下来，然后又把手放进

---

shuffle *v.* 拖着脚走
bandanna *n.* 色彩鲜艳的围巾（或头巾）

mean *adj.* 卑鄙的；自私的

into his shirt pocket and pulled out a picture.

"Give this to your grandma. Tell her there's a note on the back."

He squeezed his legs, and the horse leaped into a **gallop**. Just like that, he was gone!

And just like that I woke up sitting on the couch with my book **flopped** over in my lap.

My grandma woke up with a start. She looked over at me, smiling, and then her eyes got really big. "Where did you get that bandanna?" she asked.

I reached up and grabbed the ends of a red bandanna that was tied around my neck.

It was then that I realized that I had a picture **clutched** in my right hand. I **unfolded** it. The picture was of a handsome man sitting on a horse. I gulped and handed it to my grandma, who had big tears in her eyes.

口袋，拿出一张照片。
　　"把这个给你奶奶，告诉她后面有我写给她的话。"
　　他夹紧双腿，马向前一越，就是这样，他就消失了！
　　就是这样，我在沙发上醒来了，我的书落在我的腿上。
　　奶奶醒来吓了一跳，她笑着打量了我一下，她的眼睛睁得大大的。"你是从哪里弄来的围巾？"她问。
　　我伸手一摸，摸到了红围巾的下面，真的是有一条围巾在我的脖子上。
　　这时，我才发现我的右手里拿着一张照片，我把它打开，照片上有一个漂亮的小伙子，骑在马上。我大吸了一口气，把照片递给了奶奶，她的双眼充满了泪水。

---

gallop *n.* 飞奔；疾驰　　　　　　　　　　　flop *v.* 落下
clutch *v.* 紧握　　　　　　　　　　　　　　unfold *v.* 打开

GROWING PAINS I

I could just barely make out the writing on the back, which said, "I love you, Nettie. Always have, always will."

Well, I'm back now, and I wear the bandanna every day so I won't forget.

Sarah and Sybil don't believe my story. But who cares? They are liars and fibbers and tellers of untruth.

My diary proves it!

Besides, we are going on our third annual back-to-school picnic next week. This year it's not going to be in my back yard. We're having a real picnic in a park.

Love, Hattie MacGruder

我刚好看清照片后面的字迹，上面写着，"我爱你，内蒂，一直爱你，永远爱你！"

好的，我现在回来了，我每天都戴着这条红色的围巾，所以我不会忘记这个故事。

莎拉和塞贝尔不相信我的故事，但我才不管这些呢。她们说谎，骗人，也不说实话。

我的日记可以证明一切。

另外，下周我们要举行第三年返校野餐，今年不会在我家的后院举办了，我们会在公园里搞一个真正的野餐。

爱你的哈蒂·麦格鲁德

Max Is Angry

Max was a very angry boy. All day long, from morning until evening, he was angry. He *stomped* his feet on the ground. He kicked rocks, cans, fences, and walls. He *slammed* the drawers of his dresser, and he slammed every door he walked through.

When Max's mom asked him to take out the garbage, he made a *mean* face at her. After the fourth time she asked, he finally took out the garbage. But he *spilled* it and made a big mess on the floor.

麦柯斯生气了

麦柯斯是一个非常好生气的男孩，一整天，从早晨到晚上，他都在生气。他在地上跺脚，他踢石头、罐头盒子、篱笆，还有墙。他用力关衣橱的抽屉，走过门后使劲摔门。

妈妈让他把垃圾送到外面时，他不给妈妈好脸。妈妈说到第四遍时，他才把垃圾拿出去。但是他把垃圾弄洒了，洒了一地。妈妈要他打扫干

---

stomp v. 迈着重重地步子走
mean adj. 不善良；刻薄的

slam v. 使……砰地关上
spill v. 溢出；溅出

GROWING PAINS I

When she asked him to clean up the mess, he made another mean face.

One day Max was so angry that he kicked Dusty, the dog. Dusty *howled* in pain. From that day on, Dusty *darted* under a chair whenever he saw Max coming. Who wants to play with someone who is angry all the time?

Max's parents tried to talk with him.

"Why are you so angry?" his mom asked. Max made an angry face and stayed silent.

"What's troubling you?" his dad asked. Max only stared at the floor. Max's dad added, "Whenever you're ready to tell us, we're here to listen and help."

净，他又做出不好的脸色。

　　有一天，麦柯斯太生气了，他踢他家的狗——达斯提，达斯提疼得直叫。那天以后，达斯提看到麦柯斯来时，就像箭一样钻到椅子下面。谁想和总生气人的一起玩呢？

　　麦柯斯的爸爸妈妈想和他谈谈。

　　"为什么你总生气呢？"妈妈问他。麦柯斯满脸都是怒气，一声不吭。

　　"什么东西惹着你了？"他的爸爸问他。麦柯斯只是盯着地板。麦柯斯的爸爸接着说，"等你想要告诉我们的时候，我们就来听，也会帮助你。"

---

howl *v.* 嚎叫　　　　　　　　　　　　　　　　　　dart *v.* 飞奔；猛冲

Max went upstairs to his room and slammed the door. He threw himself on his bed, *grumbling* loudly. He buried his face in his pillow and tried to hide from the world. He didn't want to talk or think. He just wanted to be alone.

Max Begins to Think

But Max's thoughts were loud, and they kept *sneaking* into his mind. When he tried to push away the thoughts, they kept coming back stronger. Max started thinking about what his parents had said. Suddenly he felt *horrible* for having kicked Dusty. "I don't want to hurt anyone," he thought to himself.

Max got up off his bed and went back downstairs. He sat quietly at the bottom of the stairs. He wanted to ask for help, but he didn't

---

麦柯斯上了楼，回到自己的房间，把门用力地关上。他一头扎到自己的床上，大声地抱怨着。他把脸埋在枕头里面，想让自己躲开这个世界，他不想说话，也不想思考，他只想自己一个人待着。

麦柯斯开始思考

但是麦柯斯的脑子很乱，这些思想不断地钻进他的脑袋里。他不停地想把这些思想赶走，但是他们再次回来时力量更大。麦柯斯开始思考父母说过的一切。突然他感到踢达斯提让他感到很不安。"我不想伤害任何人，"他自己思考着。

麦柯斯从自己的床上起来，回到楼下。他静静地坐在楼梯下面。他想

---

grumble *v.* 发牢骚　　　　　　　　　　sneak *v.* 偷偷地走；溜
horrible *adj.* 害怕的

GROWING PAINS I

know how because he was still too angry.

When Max's parents saw him, his dad asked, "Son, would you like to talk?"

"Yes, Dad, I would," Max said.

"We're here," said his mom. "Please tell us what's going on."

Max said, "No one listens to me. At school the teacher is the boss. At home you two are the bosses. There's nowhere I'm the boss. I'm tired of always being told what to do. It makes me mad."

Max's dad smiled. "I'm glad you could tell us what you've been angry about. We're proud of you. Now, what can we do about this?"

Max's mom said, "Max, how about if you be the boss of

寻求帮助,但是他不知道怎么办,因为他现在仍然很生气。

麦柯斯的父母看到他,他爸爸问,"儿子,你想谈谈吗?"

"是的,爸爸,我想。"麦柯斯说。

"我们都在这儿,"妈妈说。"请告诉我们发生了什么事情。"

麦柯斯说,"没有人听我说话,在学校老师就是老板;在家里你们两个都是老板。在哪里我都没有说了算的时候。我烦死别人总告诉我该做什么了,这把我气坏了。"

麦柯斯的爸爸笑了,"我非常高兴你能说出让你不高兴的事情,我们为你感到骄傲,现在我们该做些什么呢?"

麦柯斯的妈妈说,"麦柯斯,如果某些事让你说了算怎么样?你想在

◆ MAX IS ANGRY

something? What would you like to be boss of?"

Max Becomes Boss

Max thought for a few minutes, and then a *grin* slowly *crept* on his face. "How about if I plan our next family vacation?"

Max's mom and dad looked at each other and nodded. Then they looked at Max and asked, "What do you have in mind?"

Max was excited. Looking happier than he had in months, he said, "I've got a great idea—we'll go on a *reptile* tour! This will be the best vacation of my life!"

哪些事上说了算?"

麦柯斯说了算

麦柯斯想了一会儿,微笑慢慢地爬上了他的脸。"如果我来计划我们家下一次假期怎么样?"

麦柯斯的妈妈和爸爸相互看了一下,点了下头。然后他们看着麦柯斯,问道,"你有什么想法呢?"

麦柯斯太高兴了,几个月来从没有这么高兴,他说,"我有一个非常好的想法——我们搞一个爬行动物旅行!这会是我一生中最好的假期了。"

---

grin *n.* 咧嘴一笑   creep *v.* 爬
reptile *n.* 爬行动物

GROWING PAINS I

Max's face lit up as he told his parents about the alligator *swamps* they would visit. Then they'd go to a zoo that raises rare snakes. They would end the trip with three days of camping near a lizard research station. "This will be the best time of my life!" Max declared with *glee*.

The next day Max was happy as he walked from school home. Even though the teacher told him what to do all day, he wasn't bothered. Even though the class *bully* was mean to him, he wasn't bothered. Finally, he was the boss of something in his life.

Someone Else Is Angry

As Max walked up the front steps to his house, he heard strange

---

麦柯斯的脸明亮起来，他告诉父母可以去鳄鱼沼泽，然后去养稀有蛇类的动物园，最后三天，他们可以在蜥蜴研究站宿营。"这会是我人生中最好的时光！"麦柯斯高兴地宣布。

第二天，麦柯斯高高兴兴地离家上学。尽管老师告诉他一天要做什么，他也没有心烦；尽管班级的老大对他非常不客气，他也没有心烦。毕竟他在他生活中的某些事情上还是说了算的。

别人生气了

麦柯斯走到自己家的台阶上时，他听到里面传出来奇怪的声音。他听

---

swamp *n.* 沼泽　　　　　　　　　　　　　　glee *n.* 欢乐；高兴
bully *n.* 恶霸；欺负弱小者

◆ MAX IS ANGRY

noises coming from inside. He heard slamming doors and angry voices. He stepped inside to see what was happening.

Max's dad was slamming drawers in the kitchen and shouting angry words that Max should not have been hearing. Max's mom was grumbling loudly as she slammed the *basement* door. They both had *nasty* looks on their faces.

Max decided to have a talk with his parents. "Why are you so angry?" he asked. Max's dad made an angry face and stayed silent.

"What's troubling you?" he asked his mom. She only looked at the floor. Max added, "Whenever you're ready to tell me, I'm here to listen and help."

到了摔门声和愤怒的说话声，他走进房间，看看发生了什么事。

爸爸在猛关厨房里的抽屉，恶狠狠地讲话，这些都不应该是麦柯斯听到的。妈妈一边使劲地摔地下室的门，一边大声抱怨。他们的脸都显得很凶恶。

麦柯斯决定与父母谈一谈。"你们为什么这么生气呢？"他问。爸爸满脸怒气，一声不出。

"什么事惹着你了？"他问妈妈，妈妈不说话只是看着地板。他又说到，"你们准备好想与我谈时，我就会来听，并且会帮助你们。"

---

basement *n.* 地下室；基地   nasty *adj.* 恶意的；凶相的

GROWING PAINS I

Max went up to his room and waited. He thought about how his parents had helped him to talk about his anger. He knew they would talk with him when they were ready.

Ready to Talk

Max's mom and dad slowly came up the stairs. They sat on the top step, looking at each other *sheepishly*. Finally, they *mustered* up the courage to knock on Max's door.

Max opened the door and saw his parents standing there with *embarrassed* looks on their faces. "Would you like to talk?" he asked.

"Yes, Max, we would," they replied.

"I'm here," said Max. "Please tell me what's going on."

麦柯斯回到房间，等待着。他在想父母曾经帮助过他关于他生气的事情，他知道他们准备好后一定会和他谈一谈的。

做好了谈话准备

麦柯斯的爸爸妈妈慢慢地来到了楼上，他们坐在楼梯的最上一个台阶上，难为情地相互看着。最后他们鼓起勇气，来敲麦柯斯的门。

麦柯斯打开了门，看到他们站在那里，满脸尴尬，"你们想谈一谈吗？"他问到。

"是的，麦柯斯，我们想谈一谈，"他们回答说。

"我就在这儿，"麦柯斯说，"请告诉我发生了什么事情吧。"

---

sheepishly *adv.* 不好意思地；难为情地   muster *v.* 鼓气；激起
embarrassed *adj.* 尴尬的；窘的

◆ MAX IS ANGRY

Max's dad said, "We want you to be in charge of something in your life. Really, we do. But we don't want to go on a *reptile* vacation. We have to *confess* that we're afraid of snakes."

Max smiled. "I'm glad you could tell me what you've been angry about. I'm proud of you. Now, what can we do about this?"

Max's mom spoke up. "How about if you go on a reptile trip with a friend? The science club *sponsors* a reptile trip every summer."

"What will you do while I'm gone?" Max asked.

Max's dad said, "We'll get some help for our fear of snakes. Maybe next year we'll be ready to *handle* a family reptile trip."

麦柯斯的爸爸说，"我们希望你为自己生活中的某些事情做主，真的，我们是这样想的。但是我们不想过爬行类动物假期，我们必须承认我们非常怕蛇。"

麦柯斯笑了，"我非常高兴，你们告诉我你们生气的原因，我为你们自豪。那么，我们应该怎样做呢？"

麦柯斯的妈妈说话了，"如果你与一个朋友一起做爬行类动物旅行呢?科学俱乐部每个暑期都会举办爬行类动物旅行的。"

"如果我不在，你们怎么办呢？"麦柯斯说。

麦柯斯的爸爸说，"怕蛇的问题我们会找别人帮忙的，非常有可能明年我们就会解决家庭爬行类动物旅行这个问题。"

---

reptile *n.* 爬行动物；爬虫
sponsor *v.* 发起；主办
confess *v.* 坦白；承认
handle *v.* 处理；管理

07

SPRAK!

A Cup of Cider

Whack! Mark sent the soccer ball sailing down his front *lawn*.

"Goooaaal!" he cheered with both arms in the air.

As he *jogged* to fetch his ball, he noticed that his neighbor, Mia, wasn't getting much business at her warm apple cider stand.

"Warm cider for sale!" Mia yelled from across the street. "Do you want some warm cider, Mark?"

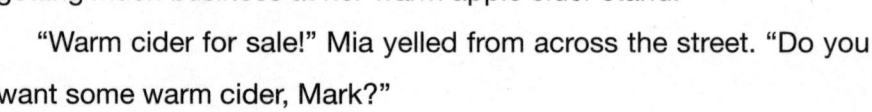

斯帕拉克！

一杯苹果汁

咔嚓！马克嗖的一脚把足球踢进了前面的草坪里面。

"加——油！"他高举双手，欢呼起来。

在他小跑着去取球的时候，他注意到他的邻居，米厄在她的热苹果汁柜台处没事儿可做。

"卖热乎乎的苹果汁了！"米厄在街对面喊着，"你想要一点儿热乎乎的苹果汁吗，马克？"

---

cider *n.* 苹果汁；苹果酒
jog *v.* 慢跑

lawn *n.* 草坪；草地

◆ SPRAK!

"No thanks!" Mark called back. Mark didn't really like warm cider. Besides, he was thirsty for a cold drink.

As Mark continued to practice for his big game the next day, he wondered about Mia's *regular* Saturday morning customers. Where were the kids, joggers and bike riders? Then he remembered that it was a holiday weekend. People are probably out of town.

After nearly an hour of *dribbling* and kicking, Mark finished his practice during which he had glanced at Mia, who never received a customer. Looking at her one last time, he went inside to get 50 cents from his mom. A few moments later, he was at Mia's stand.

"I'll take a cup of cider." Mark handed Mia the money.

"不，谢谢了！"马克向她喊道，马克不太喜欢热的苹果汁，另外他想喝冷饮。

马克继续为明天的大赛练习时，他在想着米厄周六的老顾客们。"那些孩子、慢跑的人和骑自行车的人都哪儿去了？"这时他想起来这是一个假期的周末，人们可能都不在城内。

带球、踢球快一个小时了，马克完成自己的训练了，这一段时间里他看到米厄一个顾客都没有。他又看了米厄一眼后，他回到家里，从妈妈那里要了50美分，几分钟后他来到米厄的摊位前。

"我要一杯苹果汁。"马克把钱递给了米厄。

---

regular *adj.* 经常的；固定的　　　　　dribble *v.* 带球；运球

GROWING PAINS I

"Really?" *squealed* Mia, dropping the coins into her *jar*.

"Mia!" her mother called from the front door. "Time to come inside!"

"Okay!" Mia called back to her mother before turning to back to her customer. "Thanks, Mark."

"No sweat."

A Favorite Sweater

Inside her house, Mia's mother was reading the newspaper.

"Oh goodness, it's going to get cold tomorrow night. I'm so glad your father fixed the *furnace* last weekend."

"真的?"米厄尖声尖气地说,同时把钱丢进她的坛子里。

"米厄!"她的妈妈在前门喊她,"该进屋了。"

"好的!"米厄向妈妈回了一声,然后转过身来看着这个顾客,"谢谢,马克。"

"不客气,亲爱的。"

一件最喜欢的毛衣

进到屋里,米厄的妈妈正在读报纸。

"噢,我的天呀!明天晚上会很冷的,我非常高兴,你爸爸上周把家里的壁炉修好了。"

---

squeal *v.* 尖声地说   jar *n.* 罐子;坛子
furnace *n.* 炉子;壁炉

◆ SPRAK!

Mia, still *beaming*, thought for a moment before turning to her mother.

"Mom, what about all of those people who don't have heat or any warm place to stay at all?"

"What do you mean, dear?"

Mia paused for a moment and then pulled off her sweater. "Oooh, mamma. I love this sweater. I wear it almost everyday, but it's getting too small. Maybe it's time for it to be another little girl's favorite."

Mia's mother smiled.

"I think that's an excellent idea. I'll meet you upstairs with some bags. I'm sure the *donation* center is open for a few more hours.

米厄还在高兴，想了一下后转向妈妈。

"妈妈，那些没有取暖条件或者没有暖和地方待的人可怎么办呢？"

"你什么意思呢，亲爱的？"

米厄停了一下，然后取出她的一件毛衣。"噢，妈妈，我喜欢这件毛衣，我几乎每天都穿，但它有些小了，应该让它成为另一个小女孩的最喜欢的毛衣。"

米厄的妈妈笑了。

"我看这个主意非常好，我上楼找一些袋子，我在楼上等你。我想捐赠中心的门还会开几个小时。"

---

beam *v.* 眉开眼笑；露喜气   donation *n* 捐赠物；捐赠；赠送

GROWING PAINS I

A Lost Kitten

Mia and her mother filled two bags with warm clothes and hopped in the car. On the way over to the donation center, Mia's mother slammed on the *brakes*.

"Mamma! What's wrong?"

A small kitten walked slowly in front of the car. "Do you think it's lost?" Mia continued.

"I haven't seen a house in a while. And this is a busy street. Let's take the kitten to the animal rescue center where it will be safe." Mia's mom jumped out of the car, *scooped* up the kitten, and placed it on Mia's *lap*.

一只迷路的小猫

米厄和妈妈把厚衣服装了两个大包,蹦跳着到汽车那里。在去捐赠中心的路上,米厄的妈妈突然刹车。

"妈妈!出什么事了?"

一只小猫慢悠悠地在车前走过,"你认为它迷路了吗?"米厄接着说。

"有一段时间没有看到房子了,而且这里的车还很多,我们把这只小猫送到动物救护中心吧,它在那里会安全的。"米厄的妈妈跳出汽车捧起这只小猫,把它放在米厄的膝盖上。

---

brake *n.* 刹车;制动
lap *n.* 膝部;膝盖

scoop *v.* 抱起;拣起

◆ SPRAK!

"It's so tiny!" said Mia, as she gently *stroked* the kitten. "And it's shaking!"

A Thank You Tip

"And who do you belong to, little kitty?" asked the young man from behind the desk at the rescue center. He wore a *name tag* that read, "Duane."

"We don't know," said Mia.

"It was lost on Highway 54," continued Mia's mother.

"You were right to bring it here," Duane said, scooping the kitten from Mia's arms. "We'll take good care of it. And I'm sure its owners will check in soon."

"真是太小了！"米厄说，说着她轻轻地抚摸着这只小猫，"它在发抖！"

表达感谢的小费

"你的主人是谁呢，小猫咪？"在救护中心，站在柜台后面的年轻人问。他的名字标签上写着："杜安。"

"我们不知道，"米厄说。

"它是在54号高速公路上迷路的，"米厄的妈妈说。

"你们把它带到这里是对的，"杜安说，从妈妈怀里捧过小猫。"我们会好好照顾它的，我想他的主人很快会来这里查找的。"

---

stroke *v.* 抚摸；轻轻掠过   name tag *n.* 名牌；胸佩

GROWING PAINS I

Mia and her mother felt *relieved* that the kitten was safe and off the street.

For the next several hours, Duane bathed, fed, and *soothed* the kitten. When its owners finally came for their pet, Duane and the kitten were *tangled* in a ball of *yarn*.

"Charlie!" A young boy rushed toward the kitten.

"Thank goodness he's safe," sighed the boy's mother. "And thank goodness someone found him and brought him here."

After the woman donated some money to the center for the kitten's care, she reached again for her wallet.

"Oh, no, no, no, you don't need to do that," Duane pleaded, shaking his hands in front of her. "I'm a volunteer."

小猫安全地离开了街道，米厄和妈妈也放心了。

后来的几个小时是这样的，杜安给小猫洗澡、喂东西，抚慰它。当主人来找他的宠物时，杜安和小猫正在玩线团。

"查理！"一个小孩冲向了小猫。

"谢天谢地，小猫很安全，"男孩子的妈妈长出了一口气，"感谢上帝，有人把它捡回来，并送到这里。"

女人为救护中心照顾小猫捐献了一些钱后，她又伸手拿出了钱包。

"噢，不，不用，你不用这样做。"杜安请求说，在她面前摆着手说，"我是志愿者。"

---

relieved *adj.* 放心的；宽慰的
tangle *v.* 纠缠；卷入

soothe *v.* 安抚；使平静
yarn *n.* 线；纱线

"But I insist," the woman said, "You took such good care of our Charlie." She handed Duane a tip.

A Snack

When Duane left the *shelter* that evening, he met his friends at the skating *rink*. The friends taught each other new skating moves. They raced. And they made up funky dance moves to the loud music.

"Let's take a break. Anyone up for hot *cocoa* and popcorn?" Duane asked.

At the snack bar, everyone pulled out his or her money—everyone but Rosaria.

Duane knew her family was going through some hard times, and

"但我还是要坚持这样做的，"女人说，"你对查理照顾得非常好，"她给杜安一些小费。

小吃

杜安离开救助中心的那天晚上，他到滑冰场见了几个朋友。朋友们相互传授新的滑冰动作。他们奔跑，他们伴着音乐跳着有早期布鲁斯风格的舞蹈。

"我们休息一下吧，有人想喝热可可或爆米花吗？"杜安问。

在小吃店，每个人都自己拿出钱，但是劳萨利亚没有。

杜安知道眼下她的家里经济比较困难，她没有额外吃小吃的钱。杜安

---

shelter *n.* 收容所　　　　　　　　　　　　　　　　　　rink *n.* 溜冰场
cocoa *n.* 可可粉；可可茶

she didn't have any extra money for snacks. Duane, however, did because of the tip he received from the woman at the shelter. He planned on putting it toward the digital music player he was saving up for, but Rosaria was his friend. Consequently, Duane *furtively* slipped a couple dollars into Rosaria's hand.

"Thanks," Rosaria whispered to Duane, *blushing*.

A Song

The next morning, Rosaria's mother made pancakes for breakfast. "How are my children today?" she asked her daughters.

"Great!" Rosaria *chirped*.

"Horrible," Anna *whined*. "For three weeks I've been sitting home

---

能拿出钱来，因为他在救助站里得到了那位女士的小费。他计划把这钱用在自己想买的数字音乐播放器上，但是劳萨利亚是他的朋友。于是杜安偷偷地往劳萨利亚手里塞了几美元。

"谢谢，"劳萨利亚小声对杜安说，她的脸红了。

一首歌

第二天早晨，劳萨利亚的妈妈做了薄饼早餐。

"今天我的小家伙们怎么样？"她问女儿。

"非常好！"劳萨利亚高兴地说。

"非常不好，"安娜发牢骚地说，"已经好几周了，这条骨折的腿让

---

furtively *adv.* 秘密地；鬼鬼祟祟地
chirp *v.* 轻松愉快地讲（话）

blush *v.* 脸红；感到羞愧
whine *v.* 哭诉；发牢骚

◆ SPRAK!

with this broken leg. I'm bored out of my mind. My leg *itches*. And I'm missing another soccer game!"

Rosaria's smile fell. Usually, Anna annoyed Rosaria. But today, she made Rosaria think. While she ate her pancakes in silence, she thought about how she could make Anna happy.

After breakfast, Rosaria invited Anna to her room, which was normally *off-limits*.

"Sit down, Anna. I'm going to give you a concert!" Rosaria pulled out her guitar.

"Are you serious?" Anna squealed. "You never let me hear you play!"

我只能待在家里，我很烦。我的腿痒痒的，我还不能参加接下来的足球比赛！"

劳萨利亚笑不起来了，通常安娜会让劳萨利亚心烦。但今天安娜让劳萨利亚思考了。她静静地吃着薄饼，她在想着如何能让安娜高兴起来。

吃过早餐，劳萨利亚请安娜到自己的房间里，一般的情况下这里是禁地。

"坐下吧，安娜，我给你搞一个音乐会！"劳萨利亚拿出一把吉他。

"真的吗？"安娜尖声地说，"你从不让我听你弹吉他！"

---

itch *v.* 发痒；渴望　　　　　　　off-limits *adj.* 禁止进入的

GROWING PAINS I

Rosaria played slow songs, fast songs—even a song she wrote. When the concert was over, Rosaria gave Anna one final treat: she taught her sister to play three guitar *chords*.

"With these three chords, you can play *tons* of songs," Rosaria said.

Anna was so happy, she could burst.

A Letter

Anna was so *engrossed* with the guitar concert, she nearly forgot about the soccer game she was missing. Once Rosaria left, she thought about her team and her amazing coach. So, she pulled out a piece of *stationery* and began to write.

劳萨利亚弹了慢节奏的歌，快乐节奏的歌，还有她自己写的歌，音乐会演完后，劳萨利亚给安娜一个最后的款待：她教妹妹三个吉他和弦。

"用这三个和弦，你可以弹很多很多的歌曲，"劳萨利亚说。

安娜很高兴，她都笑出声来了。

一封信

安娜对于吉他音乐会太着迷了，她几乎忘了足球比赛。劳萨利亚离开后，她想起了自己的球队，还有了不起的教练。于是，她拿出一张纸，开始写信：

---

chord *n.* 弦；和弦
engrossed *adj.* 专心致志的；全神贯注的
ton *n.* 很多；大量
stationery *n.* 信纸；信封

◆ SPRAK!

> Dear Coach Jake,
>
> I am *miserable* that I can't finish the season, but I want to thank you for teaching me so much about soccer and for showing me that I am faster and stronger and tougher than I ever thought before!
>
> See you next season,
>
> Anna

Anna *hobbled* to the mailbox in front of the house and mailed her letter.

A Blanket

That afternoon, Mark arrived early at the soccer field to practice.

> 亲爱的杰克教练，
>
> 我非常苦恼，不能完成这个赛季，但我非常感谢你教会我很多关于足球的知识，感谢你让我知道，我比自己以前认为的更快、更强、更勇敢！
>
> 下个赛季再见。
>
> 安娜

安娜跛着脚来到房前的邮筒，把这封信寄出了。

一条毯子

那天下午，马克很早就到了足球场练习，他的爸爸、奶奶也来观看比

---

miserable *adj.* 痛苦的；苦恼的　　　　　　hobble *v.* 跛行；蹒跚

GROWING PAINS I

His dad and grandmother came to watch the game.

"Hey, Mark. Hello, Mr. James. And who is this?" Coach Jake held his hand out for Mark's grandmother to *shake*.

"Hello, dear," Grandma smiled. "I've heard so much about you, Coach Jake."

"No kidding? Well, I'm glad you could make it. Mark is quite a player, you know." Coach Jake paused, then looked closer at Grandma. "Are you cold, ma'am? You're *shivering*!"

"You know, dear, I am a bit chilly," Grandma said.

"Hold on a second," Coach Jake dashed to his car.

赛。

"嗨,马克。你好,詹姆斯先生。这位是……?" 杰克教练把手伸向奶奶,与她握手。

"你好,亲爱的," 奶奶笑着说,"别人总与我提到你,杰克教练。"

"不是开玩笑的吧?嗯,我非常高兴你能来看比赛,马克的球踢得很好,你知道的。" 杰克教练停了一下,然后仔细地看看奶奶,"你冷吗,女士?你有些发抖!"

"你知道,亲爱的,我是有些冷," 奶奶说。

"请等一下," 杰克教练快速走向他的汽车。

---

shake *v.* 握手　　　　　　　　　　　　　　　shiver *v.* 颤抖;发抖

♦ SPRAK!

When he returned, he placed a *plaid* wool blanket on Grandma's lap.

"Well, are't you thoughtful ! I sure do appreciate this, Coach," Grandma said with a big smile.

SPRAK!

"Thanks for doing that for my grandma, Coach Jake."

Mark and Coach Jake jogged out to the field to practice.

"Hey, it was nothing. I'm in the mood to SPRAK," Coach Jake replied.

"You're in the mood to what?" Mark asked.

他回来的时候,他把一个方格子毛毯盖在了奶奶的腿上。

"嗯,你可真会关心人!我真是太感激你了,教练先生,"奶奶开心地笑着说。

斯帕拉克!

"谢谢你为我奶奶做了这些,杰克教练。"

马克和杰克教练跑着到球场练习去了。

"喂,这没有什么,我的心情是斯帕拉克的状态,"杰克教练回答说。

"你的心情是什么状态?"马克问。

---

plaid *adj.* 有格子图案的

GROWING PAINS I

"You know—SPRAK. Spread *Random* Acts of Kindness. It feels good to think about others."

"I've never heard of SPRAK," laughed Mark.

"I see you SPRAK all the time, man! Remember last week when that little kid dropped his warm *pretzel* and cried? You went over and made him laugh. And a few weeks ago when it was warm, you poured water into a cup so that dog got a drink. I felt like spreading some kindness today, too." Coach Jake *head-butted* the ball to Mark.

"Cool," Mark said as he caught the ball on his foot and dribbled toward the goal.

"Yeah. It is cool to SPRAK. Now let's see what you've got!"

"你知道——斯帕拉克，Spread Random Acts of Kindness（到处传播爱心），想着别人让人很舒服。"

"我从来没有听说过斯帕拉克，"马克笑了。

"我看你总在斯帕拉克，小伙子！你还记着上周一个小孩把自己的热乎乎的椒盐脆饼掉了时哭的事儿吗？你走过去，把他给弄笑了。还有几周前，天气还不冷的时候，你把水倒进了杯子里，狗就可以喝到水了。我今天也非常想传播友爱。"杰克教练把球顶给马克。

"好球，"马克用脚接住球说，然后把球带到球门。

"是的，斯帕拉克也很酷，现在我们看一下你收获了什么！"

---

random *adj.* 任意的；随意的　　　　pretzel *n.* 椒盐卷饼；椒盐脆饼干
head-butted *v.* 用头撞击；头击

◆ ELEVENTEEN

Eleventh

Eleventeen

Sarah turned eleventh yesterday, which made it a very special day. A person can turn eleventh only once, and most people never turn eleventh at all.

In fact, I'll let you in on a little secret. Sarah is the only person who has ever turned eleventh. Ever! Not a *single* other living *soul* has done it. Not a single other dead soul has done it either.

You're probably wondering how Sarah *accomplished* this rare and *extraordinary* feat. This, of course, is that story.

11岁

莎拉昨天11岁了,这使得昨天非常与众不同。一个人一生中只有一次11岁,有些人一辈子都不可能有11岁。

实际上是我想让你了解一个小小的秘密,莎拉是唯一的一个到了11岁的人。从未有过!没有一个活着的人能做到这一点,其他死了的人也没能做到过这一点。

你可能在想莎拉是怎样完成这个少见而超常的绝活儿的。这个,当然了,就是那个故事了。

---

single *adj.* 单一的;单个的
accomplish *v.* 完成;实现

soul *n.* 人;家伙
extraordinary *adj.* 特别的;非凡的

GROWING PAINS I

"I'm bored," said Sarah, as she walked into the kitchen for breakfast one Saturday morning.

"Would you like to invite a friend over?" asked her mother.

"No," said Sarah, "that's not the problem. I'm bored being ten."

"Well, your birthday is only a few weeks away," said her mother, "so you won't have to be ten much longer."

"I'm bored being eleven," Sarah said.

"You've never even been eleven!" *interjected* her big sister, Kate, entering the room. "I guess you want to be a teenager, just like me."

"我有些心烦，"莎拉说，这是一个星期六的早晨，她走进厨房吃早餐。

"你想不想请一个朋友过来？"她妈妈问她。

"不了，"莎拉说，"这不是问题，问题是我对10岁这个年龄很烦。"

"好吧，你的生日过几周就到了，"妈妈说，"所以你的10岁很快就过去了。"

"我到了11岁也会很烦的，"莎拉说。

"你不会永远11岁的！"她的大姐姐，凯特，边走进屋边插话说，"我猜你想当青少年，就像我这样。"

---

interject *v.* 打断（别人的讲话）；插话

♦ ELEVENTEEN

"I want to be like you about as much as I want to be a *snail*," Sarah *retorted*, proud that she could think of a *comeback* so quickly.

"Well, that's funny because you are as slow as one," said Kate.

Uh-oh. Sarah needed another comeback, quick, and she didn't have one on the tip of her tongue. Her eight-year old brother, Noah—as usual, at the breakfast table before anyone else—saved her.

"I wish you were both eighteen," Noah said. "Why?" asked Mom.

"Because then they'd both go away to college, and I'd have Mommy all to myself."

"我想像你一样,与我想当蜗牛是一样的,"莎拉反驳说,对自己的回马枪杀得这么快很自豪。

"好吧,这很有趣儿,因为你慢得真像一个蜗牛,"凯特说。

呵,噢。莎拉还需要一个回马枪,要很快的,但她的嘴边儿没有了,她8岁的弟弟,诺亚(和平常一样,总是在别人之前在餐桌前坐好)救了她。

"我希望你们都是18岁,"诺亚说。

"为什么呢,"妈妈问。

"因为,到那时,你们都去上大学了,妈妈只属于我一个人的了。"

---

snail n. 蜗牛;迟钝的人   retort v. 反驳;反击
comeback n. 反驳;反唇相讥

GROWING PAINS I

"What about Daddy?" asked Sarah.

"What about me?" Dad said as he walked into the kitchen, opening the newspaper and not looking where he was going.

Noah *smirked* and "*humphed*", as if to say that everyone knows dads are not nearly the problem that big sisters are.

"Sarah's bored being ten," Mom said to Dad. He looked up and noticed everyone looking at him.

"Well, her birthday is only a few weeks away," he said brightly, as if he were sure he had this one figured out. "She won't have to be ten much longer," he concluded.

"那爸爸呢？"莎拉问。

"我怎么了？"爸爸走进厨房，边走边说，同时打开报纸，也没看往哪里走。

诺亚傻笑着，还"表示不满"，好像是说，每个人都知道爸爸与大姐姐相比，不算是个大问题。

"莎拉不喜欢10岁这个年龄，"妈妈对爸爸说，他抬起头，发现大家都在看着他。

"好吧，她的生日还有几周就到了，"他欢快地说，好像是他非常确定他已经计算好了一样。"她10岁的时间不会有太久了，"他最后说。

---

smirk *v.* 傻笑；假笑   humph *v.* 发哼声

◆ ELEVENTEEN

"We've been thought that," Sarah and Kate said *in unison*.

"Oh," Dad said, "so what's wrong with being eleven?"

"It's too far away from eighteen," said Noah.

"So what's the big rush to be eighteen?" asked Dad, clearly confused.

"Oh, never mind," Sarah said, getting up from the table.

"Aren't you going to eat your breakfast?" Mom asked.

"I'm not hungry," Sarah said.

"Right," piped in Kate, her voice *dripping* with adolescent *sarcasm*, "she's too busy being bored to be hungry."

"我们已经想过这件事儿了，"莎拉和凯特一起说。

"噢，"爸爸说，"那11岁有什么不好呢？"

"那离18岁还很远呢，"诺亚说。

"那么为什么要急于到18岁呢？"爸爸问，很明显他是被搞糊涂了。

"噢，不要在意，"莎拉说着站了起来。

"你想不想吃早餐了？"妈妈问。

"我还不饿呢，"莎拉说。

"好的，"凯特提高声音说道，她的嗓音带有青少年特有的讽刺，"她心烦得很，没有时间饿了。"

---

in unison 一起；一致地　　　　　　　　　　drip *v.* 充满；充溢
sarcasm *n.* 讽刺；挖苦

63

GROWING PAINS 1

"Kate, you're being mean!" said Sarah, storming out of the kitchen. As she left, she heard her father say, for the millionth time, "Kate, be nice to Sarah."

Sarah went to her room. She needed some *silence*, some time to think. She had to admit that anything that ended with "teen" sounded better than anything that didn't. "Eleven" isn't bad, really. At least it has more than one *syllable*. But then Sarah realized she'd have to spend a whole year being twelve, and twelve sounded just *awful*. Nothing very exciting could happen to someone called "twelve," she supposed. She needed to be a teenager, but that was too far away even to think about. It was a *dilemma*, no doubt about that.

"凯特，你这个坏东西！"莎拉说着从厨房里冲了出来。她出来的时候，听见爸爸说，"凯特，对莎拉好一点儿，"这样说已经是第一百万遍了。

莎拉朝自己的房间走去，她需要安静一下，需要一点时间思考一下。她必须承认，以有"teen"结尾的东西比没有的好。"11"没有毛病，的确是的。至少它不仅只是一个音节。但是莎拉想起来，她还要在12岁过上一年，12这个词听起来很不好听。一个人被称为12，是不可能遇上让人非常兴奋的事情的，她想。她想成为一个青年，但离得还太远，甚至想一想都觉得远，这真是一件矛盾的事儿，这一点毫无疑问。

---

silence *n.* 沉默状态；无声状态

awful *adj.* 糟糕的；糟透的

syllable *n.* 音节

dilemma *n.* （进退两难的）窘境，困境

◆ ELEVENTEEN

Whenever Sarah had a dilemma, her father would tell her to "weigh the facts." She was never sure whether he was kidding or thought dilemmas really could be solved by putting facts on some kind of *scale*. Anyway, she'd never weighed the facts. But then, she'd never solved any dilemmas, either. Maybe there was something to Dad's advice.

Sarah took out her drawing *pad* and two colored pencils. She decided a table would be her scale to weigh the facts. The first column was *labeled* "being a teenager" and was in *lavender* because it would be wonderful to be a teenager. The second column was labeled "being eleven" and was in royal blue because the color was full of possibilities.

每当莎拉遇到矛盾时，她的爸爸就会告诉她"权衡事实。"她从没有弄明白他是开玩笑，还是真的认为把事实放在秤上称一称就能解决矛盾。不管怎么说，她从没有权衡过事实，但她也从来没解决好过任何矛盾，也许爸爸的建议还有一些道理。

莎拉拿出自己的图画本和两支彩色铅笔，她想做一个表来作为她权衡这些事实的秤。第一栏标上"当一个青少年"，用淡紫色，因为当青少年是一件非常美妙的事情。第二栏标上"在11岁"，用蓝色，因为这种颜色充满了可能性。

---

scale *n.* 天平；称　　　　　　　　　pad *n.* 便笺本；拍纸簿
label *v.* 标注；贴标签于　　　　　　lavender *n.* 淡紫色；薰衣草

GROWING PAINS I

The whole rest of the page was *blank*. Sarah started thinking about teenagers and eleven-year-olds so she could decide what to write. She wanted to list all the good things about being a teenager and all the good things about being eleven. She could then *compare* the good things about each age and see which was better.

The first thing she put in the teenager column was: can go to *mall* by myself. That was a good one because Sarah most *definitely* could not go to the mall by herself. She kept making entries, and finally the table looked like this:

Being a teenager

Can go to mall by myself

Can babysit to earn money

Being Eleven

Can walk to park with Alika

Can babysit for Noah

这页的其他部分都留出空白，莎拉开始想关于青少年和十一岁的问题，然后就可以决定要写什么了。她想把所有关于青少年的好的方面列出来，再把所有关于十一岁的好的方面列出来。然后她把两个年龄好的方面比较一下，看看哪一个更好。

她在青少年这一栏里写的是：可以自己去购物中心，这是一件好事，因为莎拉真的不能自己去购物中心。她继续列出内容，最后这个表就像下面的样子：

当一个青少年，可以自己去购物中心。当他十岁时，可以和阿利卡一起去公园替人看小孩挣钱。

---

blank *adj.* 空白的；未写过的
mall *n.* 购物商场

compare *v.* 对照；比较
definitely *adv.* 明确地；肯定地

◆ ELEVENTEEN

Sarah started to think about what she'd put in the "being eleven" column. Now that she was turning eleven, she would have more *responsibility* for herself and others.

She and Alika, her best friend, would be able to jog down to the park to play soccer. They could go any time they wanted as long as it was before dark and they told their parents where they were going. Sarah was a good *athlete*, one of the fastest kids in class, and great at the standing long jump. The park was more fun than the mall. But she had been dying to go to the mall by herself.

It was definitely exciting to be able to go to the mall without your parents or your big sister. The few times that Kate had taken Sarah to the mall, she had made Sarah feel as though she was even younger than ten. Sarah had big dreams about walking into stores

---

莎拉开始想她要在"在11岁"这个栏里加什么。现在马上就要到11岁了,她对自己和其他人要有更多的责任。

她和阿利卡,她最好的朋友,可以小跑到公园去踢足球,只要天没有黑,并且告诉父母去处,她们只要想去就能去。莎拉的体育非常好,是全班跑得最快的,站立跳远也是非常好的。公园比购物中心更有意思,但是她非常想自己去购物中心。

没有父母或大姐姐陪着,自己去购物中心绝对是令人兴奋的事情。凯特只是很少几次带她去过购物中心,但是她让莎拉感觉自己是一个10岁不到的孩子,莎拉的一个很大的梦想就是能像一个很酷的青少年一样,走进

---

responsibility *n.* 责任;职责   athlete *n.* 运动员

GROWING PAINS 1

as a cool teenager. She would choose how long she stayed at each store, which store to go to next, or to stay another ten minutes just looking at the kittens.

As Sarah looked down her table's columns, she began to realize something. She liked *babysitting* because she could *earn* money. Sixteen-year-olds got to babysit all the time. When Sarah turned eleven, her parents said she could babysit Noah and they would pay her. She would still be too young to babysit other people's children, but at least she could babysit Noah. Sarah thought that in that way, she would be close to being sixteen. At eleven she could babysit Noah and earn money and buy the things she wanted, like blue *nail* polish.

商店。她可以决定在每个店里停留的时间，然后去哪个商店，或者再待上10分钟看看小猫。

莎拉看着桌子上面的表格，她开始意识到一件事情。她喜欢照看小孩，因为这会让她挣到钱。16岁的人可以一直照看小孩。莎拉到了11岁时，她的父母说，她能够照看诺亚，而且会给她付工资。看别人的孩子对她来说，她的年龄还有些小，但是她至少可以看诺亚，挣到钱可以买自己想要的东西，例如蓝色的指甲油。

---

babysit *v.* 替人临时照看（小孩）　　　　　　　　　　earn *v.* 获得；挣得
nail *n.* 指甲

♦ ELEVENTEEN

In fact, that was another way she would be like a sixteen-year-old. She could use her own money and buy things she wanted. It wasn't like an *allowance*, with her parents still saying yes or no to what she bought. She would earn the money so the decisions about what she could spend it on would be hers—just like a sixteen-year-old.

Sarah *completed* the last line in the table: can spend my money on what I want. Then it was there in lavender and blue. At eleven, she would be a whole lot closer to being sixteen than she was at ten. Actually, if you look at it one way, eleven was only five words away from sixteen. That's when it dawned on her.

Can go to mall by myself   Can walk to park with Alika
Can babysit to earn money   Can babysit for Noah
Can spend my money on what I want

实际上，她喜欢16岁还有另一个原因，她可以用自己的钱买自己想要的东西，这与零花钱不同，那需要父母对于她要买的东西说是否同意。她要挣钱，这样决定钱如何花是她自己说了算，就像16岁的人一样。

莎拉完成了这个表格的最后一行，"能按自己的要求花钱。"这样一切都写好了，有淡紫色和蓝色的。到了11岁，就会比10岁更接近16岁了。实际上如果你用一种方式来看这个问题，11岁离16岁只有5个单词的距离，这样她就快见到曙光了。

可以自己去购物中心   可以和阿利卡走着去公园
可以看小孩挣钱   可以照看诺亚挣钱
可以按自己的想法花钱

---

allowance n. 零花钱；生活费   complete v. 完成；结束

GROWING PAINS I

Eleventeen! That's what she would be! Like a teenager—*responsible*, able to earn money, and make her own decisions about how to spend it—but not yet a teenager in years. Besides, she thought, it's more important to act older than to be older. Her dad was right—when you have a dilemma, all you have to do is weigh the facts.

Sarah knew people might ask her what she meant when she told them she's eleventeen, but that was no problem. She would tell them, "Oh, someday you'll find out, when you're eleventeen."

But of course they wouldn't, because no one had ever been eleventeen before, and probably no one would ever be again!

11岁！她就要达到的年龄！和青少年一样，有一定的责任，能够挣钱，还能决定怎样花钱——但几年内还不算是一个青少年。而且，她想，更重要的是表现老练一些，比真正老要好一些。她的爸爸是对的，如果遇到矛盾，你必须做的事情，就是权衡事实。

莎拉知道，当她告诉别人她11岁时，别人会问她什么意思，但这不算是一个问题。她会告诉他们，"噢，将来有一天你们就会明白的，当你11岁时。"

但是他们不会问的，因为以前没有人有过11岁，也可能没有人能再过一次11岁！

---

responsible *adj.* 有责任的；负责的

09

Becky's Puzzle Problem

Becky Finds the Perfect *Puzzle*

It was a *gloomy*, rainy Saturday, but even so, Becky was very excited. Today was the day she would be picking out a new puzzle—a birthday gift from Mom and Dad.

Becky was a "puzzle person," or so her mom said. She had started with baby-size wooden ones, *progressed* to 50 pieces, then 100, and then 200. Now it would be a bigger challenge, her first

---

贝吉的拼图问题

贝吉发现一个最好的拼图

这个周六天是灰暗的,还下着雨,尽管如此,贝吉仍旧很兴奋,因为今天她要选一个新的拼图,这是妈妈爸爸要送她的生日礼物。

贝吉是一个"拼图狂人",妈妈就是这么说的。最开始她用的是婴儿适用的木制拼图,然后是50块的,100块的,后来是200块的。这一次将

---

puzzle *n.* 谜;智力游戏　　　　　　gloomy *adj.* 阴暗的;幽暗的
progress *v.* 前进;进步

GROWING PAINS I

300-piece puzzle. And even better, she had a three-day weekend ahead to put it together.

At the toy shop, she was *overwhelmed* with the *array* of puzzles. Some had as many as 9,000 pieces! At last, she found the 300-piece puzzle *section*, and saw one she liked.

"Mom, I found it," Becky said. "Right here, the one with the animals." It was beautiful—a painting of African *wild* animals near a watering hole. A snowy mountain was in the background, and birds were flying around. "It's neat because you can see the whole picture in the water, too," she said. "It's like having two puzzles in one."

是更大的挑战——她的第一个300块拼图，而且更好的是，她还将有一个三天的周末，可以用来拼这个拼图。

到了玩具店，一排排拼图让她眼花缭乱，有的居然有9000块！最后她找到了一个300块的拼图区，看到一个她喜欢的。

"妈妈，我找到了，"贝吉说，"就在这里，这个有动物的。"这个很漂亮，画的是非洲野生动物，聚集在一个水塘边。背景是覆盖积雪的大山，鸟儿在周围飞翔。"这个真好，因为还可以在水中看到这个图（倒影），"她说，"好像有两个拼图一样。"

---

overwhelm *v.* 使不知所措；压垮
section *n.* 地区

array *n.* 排列；列阵
wild *adj.* 野生的

◆ BECKY'S PUZZLE PROBLEM

At home, she carefully cleared off the large dining room table and *measured* the area the puzzle would cover. The box said 16 by 24 inches.

Becky carefully *dumped* the pieces out onto the table, and turned them over, right side up. This took a little time, and she was impatient to get going. "This does look like a lot more pieces," she said. In fact, there were twice as many pieces as the last puzzle she completed.

It's All in How You Look at It

First, she searched for straight edges to make a *frame* for the picture. Some of these pieces were easy to *spot*; others had just a

---

回到家,她认真地把大大的餐桌收拾干净,量出拼图需要的地方。盒子上说是16乘24英寸。

贝吉把这些拼图小心地倒在桌子上,把它们翻过来,正面向上。这花了不少时间,他想拼图已经急不可耐了。"这看起来的确有些块数太多了,"她说。事实上,这是她上次完成拼图数量的两倍。

一切在于你怎样看

首先,她寻找直线边缘的图块,做出图片的外框。其中有一些图块非常容易找到,还有一些小小的线条边儿。然后她找可以放在一起的图

---

measure *v.* 测量;计量　　　　　　　　　　　dump *v.* 倾倒
frame *n.* 构架　　　　　　　　　　　　　　　spot *v.* 找出;认出

GROWING PAINS I

teeny-weeny bit of a straight edge. Then she began to spot pieces that might go together... pieces of a tree... the zebra's *stripes*... the *distinctive* marks of the *giraffe*. Those pieces she put together in little piles off to the side. She was getting organized! By lunchtime, Becky had two sides completed.

Later that afternoon, her dad came and sat down next to her. "How's it going?" he asked, as he picked up a piece. "Okay," Becky said, "but this is taking longer than I expected."

"I always look for shape first," Dad said. "It's a trick I learned from my father."

Becky looked up at her dad. "Grandpa John?" Try as she might, Becky could not imagine her father as a little boy doing a puzzle with

---

块……树的图块……斑马的条纹……长颈鹿的标志性记号。她把这些小块放在一边儿，堆在一起。她越来越有条理！到了午餐时，贝吉已经完成了两条边儿。

后来那天下午，她的爸爸来了，坐在她的身旁。"进展如何？"他问，同时拿起了一块拼图。"很好，"贝吉说，"但花的时间会比我预想的要长一些。"

"我总会先找形状，"爸爸说，"这是我跟我的爸爸学来的技巧。"

贝吉招起头看着爸爸，"约翰爷爷？"尽管贝吉使劲地想着爸爸儿时与爷爷一起玩拼图的样子，她就是想不出来。

---

stripe *n.* 条纹；斑纹　　　　distinctive *adj.* 有特色的；与众不同的
giraffe *n.* 长颈鹿

◆ BECKY'S PUZZLE PROBLEM

Grandpa.

Dad said, "I put all the ones with the *loop* out over here, and the long ones over here." Well now, that was news to Becky! She had never considered shape as a way to *separate* pieces. He continued, "This way when you need one like this," he held up a squarish piece, "it will be here in this pile."

Dad pushed his piece in place, and said, "Got one!"

Becky Hits a *Snag*

Now things were moving along better; the giraffe's head was easy. But then Becky hit a snag—too many grassy areas that all looked alike. Even the shape trick wasn't working. She was getting

---

爸爸说，"我把所有带环的放在那边儿，把长的放在这边儿。"噢，好的，这对于贝吉来说还是第一次听到！她从来没有想过利用形状把这些拼图块区分开。他接着说，"如果你需要一个这样的话，你就用这种方法，"他拿起呈正方形的一块拼图。"它就会在这边儿的堆里。"

爸爸把一块拼图放进合适的位置，然后说，"搞定一个！"

贝吉遇到了一个麻烦

现在事情进展得很顺利，长颈鹿的头很好弄。但是这时贝吉遇到了一个麻烦——有太多的草地了，看起来都是一样的。就是形状窍门也不好用。她有些累了、饿了，也有些失去信心了。这一天过得太快了，雨已经

---

loop *n.* 圈；环
snag *n.* 障碍；麻烦

separate *v.* 分开；分离

GROWING PAINS I

tired, hungry, and a little *discouraged*. The day had gone by fast. The rain had stopped, and it was dark outside.

"Time for dinner, Becky," called Mom. "Your favorite, *macaroni* and cheese."

Mom looked at Becky closely. "You look unhappy, Becky. Something wrong?" Becky admitted this puzzle was much harder than she expected. Her head hurt from working on it all day.

"Well," Mom said, "after dinner, we'll take a look at it together."

After dinner, they pulled up another chair, and moved the table over a bit so they could all sit together. Becky was now looking at the puzzle upside down, and immediately saw three pieces that fit! This was great! "Hey, look, just moving over here gave me a different

---

停了，外面都已经黑了。

"该吃晚饭了，贝吉，"妈妈叫她。"是你最爱吃的通心面与起司。"

妈妈仔细地看了看贝吉，"你看起来有些不高兴呀，贝吉，有什么事儿吗？"贝吉承认这个拼图比预想的难得多，拼了一整天她的头有些疼。

"好吧，"妈妈说，"吃完晚饭后，我们一起去看看。"

吃完晚饭，他们把椅子拉到一起，搬了一下桌子，这样大家就可以坐在一起。贝吉现在从反面看着这个拼图，她马上就看出来有三块拼图很合适，这真是一个好办法！"喂，看呀，倒过来看以后，我发现我找到合适

---

discouraged *adj.* 气馁的；泄气的   macaroni *n.* 通心面

way to see where the pieces fit."

The Dream

That night, Becky dreamed about the puzzle. Big *lopsided* pieces were floating in space, and would not organize themselves! Straight edges, loops, and colors were all mixed up. She woke in the morning, feeling *unsure* about this whole puzzle thing. Maybe she should just cool it for a while, she thought.

That afternoon, they all went to the gym to exercise and swim laps in the pool. Becky swam as fast as she could, completing two laps to her parents' one. She was feeling very *energetic*! For a while, Becky completely forgot about her dream and the puzzle. When they

---

位置的方式了。"

做梦

那天晚上，贝吉梦到了拼图，大大的歪斜的拼图块在空中飘着，就是乱乱地不拼在一起！直线的边儿、环状边和各种颜色都搅在一起。她早晨起来，被这些拼图搞得不知所措。"也许应该把这件事放下一段时间，"她想。

那天下午，他们一起去体育馆锻炼身体，在游泳池中游了好几圈。贝吉使出了全身的力气游，爸爸妈妈游一圈儿，她就游两圈儿。她感到精力非常旺盛！在很长的一段时间，贝吉完全忘了她做过的梦和拼图的事儿。

---

lopsided *adj.* 不平衡的；向一侧倾斜的   unsure *adj.* 不确定的
energetic *adj.* 精力充沛的

GROWING PAINS I

all returned home, she was *eager* to start her puzzle again.

Another Point of *View*

On Sunday, one of Becky's best friends, Sara, came over to play. Sara was a good puzzler, too. "Becky, you need to get all these shades of blue over here, see?" Becky did see, but the blues were sky and water. Still, Sara's idea was worth trying. And there were still lots and lots of pieces to go.

Now Becky and Sara had several ways to work: by straight edge (the easy one), by *design*, by shape, by looking at the puzzle upside down and sideways, and by color.

回到了家中时,她又想做拼图了。

另一个角度看事物

周日那天,贝吉的一个好朋友,萨拉过来玩了。萨拉也是一个拼图高手。"贝吉,你应该把这种蓝色放在那边儿,你知道吗?"贝吉真的明白了,但蓝色有的是天空,有的是水。但是萨拉的想法还是值得试一试的,而且还有很多很多的拼图块要拼的。

现在贝吉和萨拉有好几种方法了:用直边的办法(最容易的)、用图案的方法、用形状的方法、从反面看的方法、从侧面看的方法和看颜色的方法。

---

eager *adj.* 渴望的;热切的 view *n.* 观察;意见
design *n.* 设计;图案

◆ BECKY'S PUZZLE PROBLEM

Even with all the puzzle tricks, there were times when the two of them couldn't find the right piece. Sara even tried standing on her head. And believe it or not, that worked, too!

An *Unexpected* Problem

By Monday morning, the puzzle was nearly complete. By Monday afternoon, less than ten pieces were left, and Becky was starting to celebrate! It was a beautiful picture... but wait... a piece was missing! MISSING! Becky looked on the floor, on the *couch*, even under the puzzle.

"Mom! Dad!" she hollered, "a piece is MISSING!"

They *combed* through every inch of the dining room and kitchen.

用尽了所有的这些方法，有时还会剩下两块找不到合适的位置，萨拉甚至试过倒立的方法了，不管你信不信，这种方法也是很有效的。

一个没有预见到的问题

星期一的早晨，拼图就要完成了，周一的下午，只剩下十块左右了，贝吉都快要庆祝自己的胜利了！这是一幅漂亮的图画……但请等一下……有一块拼图不知哪里去了，丢了！贝吉在地上找、在沙发上找、甚至把拼图下面都找过了。

"妈妈、爸爸！"她大喊道，"有一块拼图找不到了。"

他们把起居室和厨房的每一寸的地方都找过了，他们找过了地毯下

---

unexpected *adj.* 意外的；意想不到的　　　　couch *n.* 躺椅；长沙发椅
comb *v.* 到处搜寻；彻底搜查

GROWING PAINS I

They checked under the rug, in back of the bookcase, underneath the couch cushions—no puzzle piece anywhere.

Becky's mouth was turned down. A *defective* puzzle! Who would have known? It wasn't 300 pieces, it was 299!

"Okay, Becky, I have an idea," said Dad.

Dad to the Rescue

They carefully *glued* the finished puzzle onto poster board, and hung it next to the other four in Becky's bedroom. The missing piece wasn't even noticeable. They had found a little picture of their cat, Snowball, and cut it into the shape of the missing piece. The face of Snowball peered out where the baby lion's face was supposed to be in the puzzle. Little Snowball didn't look nearly as *ferocious*.

面、书柜的后面、沙发靠垫下面，就是哪里都找不到这块拼图。

贝吉的嘴角都垂落下来了。一个有毛病的拼图！谁知道呢？这不是300块，这是299块！

"好吧，贝吉，我有一个主意，"爸爸说。

爸爸过来救援

他们仔细地把完成的拼图粘在一个宣传板上，与贝吉屋内的以前的4个拼图挂在一起，缺少的那块拼图几乎是看不出来的。他们找到了他们小猫"雪球"的一张小照片，把这张照片剪成丢掉的那块的形状。雪球的脸放在原本拼图中幼狮脸的地方。小雪球看起来没有那么凶猛。

---

defective adj. 不完美的；有缺陷的   glue v. 黏合；粘贴
ferocious adj. 凶猛的；残忍的

◆ BECKY'S PUZZLE PROBLEM

So, it looked really neat, after all. And Becky was very proud of her dad for coming up with such a *brilliant* idea!

A Surprise Ending

On Tuesday, Becky was scrambling to get ready for school. She found the missing puzzle piece in the *cuff* of her jeans. *Stunned*, she looked at it. Now that Snowball was in the picture, what should she do? She quickly compared the two pieces, and decided she liked her *version* better. She taped the missing piece to the edge of the finished puzzle. It was a reminder that sometimes creative puzzle solving is more than just getting pieces to fit.

就这样，拼图终究看起来比较整齐了，贝吉以爸爸想出的这个巧妙的想法而非常自豪。

令人惊喜的结局

周二，贝吉正在急着准备上学，她在牛仔裤的裤腿中找到了丢失的那块拼图块。她非常惊讶地看着这块拼图，"现在雪球已经被安到了里面，它该怎么办呢？"她快速地把两个拼图块比较了一下，认为她更喜欢自己的想法。她把找到的这块拼图贴在拼好的拼图边儿上。把它作为一种提示：有时创造性的方法解决拼图问题比单纯地把拼图拼起来更加有意义。

---

brilliant *adj.* 巧妙的，杰出的　　　　　cuff *n.* 裤脚的翻边；袖口
stun *v.* 使大吃一惊　　　　　　　　　　version *n.* 版本

GROWING PAINS I

10

Alice's Birthday Cake

Chapter One

Alice had a wonderful dream. It was her thirteenth birthday. Her mother had baked her a cake with pink *frosting*. Her father was handing her a brightly *wrapped* box with a beautiful bow.

Alice woke up just as she was *unwrapping* the present. She *snapped* her eyes shut, hoping to slip back into the lovely dream, but it was too late. She could hear her mother getting ready for work. Alice glanced at the clock on the table next to her bed. It was time

爱丽丝的生日蛋糕

第一章

爱丽丝做了一个甜美的梦。她13岁生日的时候,妈妈亲手做了一个用粉色糖霜装饰的蛋糕。爸爸正把一个系有漂亮蝴蝶结,包装精美的盒子递给她。

当她正要打开礼物的时候,梦醒了。她使劲地闭上眼睛,希望能回到那个甜美的梦中,但是太晚了,她听到妈妈正准备去上班。爱丽丝看了看床头桌上的闹钟。她也该起床了。

---

frosting *n.* 糖霜混合物
unwrap *v.* 打开
wrapped *adj.* 有包装的
snap *v.* 把……一下子打开(或关闭)

for her to get up, too.

Alice's room remained dark as she dressed because heavy *blackout* curtains sealed out the golden sunlight. The country was deep into World War II, and people were afraid that *enemy* planes would see lights from the city and know where to drop their bombs. Every night, outdoor lights were turned off and indoor lights were hidden. A warden *patrolled* Alice's neighborhood each night. He made sure not even a sliver of light *glowed* around the edges of drawn blackout curtains.

Alice looked forward to pushing aside her blackout curtains each morning to let sunlight flood her room. This morning Alice felt cheerful. She might play in the park after school with her friends. But first she had to wake her little brother, Robert, get him dressed, give

---

当她穿衣服时，房间还是很黑，因为厚厚的不透光窗帘挡住了明媚的阳光。这个国家正处在二战中，人们担心敌机看到光亮，从城市上空投掷炸弹。每天晚上，户外的灯被熄灭，室内的灯光也隐藏起来。每天晚上，都有一名管理人员在爱丽丝家附近巡逻。他要确保连被拉下的窗帘边缘也不透一丝光亮。

每天早晨，爱丽丝都期待着拉开那不透光的窗帘，好让阳光洒满房间。今天早晨，爱丽丝很高兴。她可以在放学后和朋友在花园里玩耍。但首先，她要叫醒弟弟罗伯特，帮他穿上衣服，为他准备早餐，然后送他去上学。

---

blackout *n.* 不透光窗罩（或窗帘）　　enemy *n.* 敌人；敌军
patrol *v.* 巡逻；巡查　　glow *v.* 发出微弱而稳定的光

GROWING PAINS 1

him breakfast, and walk him to school.

Alice's mother had already left for work by the time Alice and Robert walked into the kitchen. After Alice's father had been shipped out to fight the war in Europe, Alice's mother took a job working at a factory that made parts for ships. Like many women, she held a job once done by a man who had been shipped out like Alice's father. America needed new ships to win the war, and it was up to the women to work eight to twelve hour days, six or seven days a week to keep the factories running.

Alice was proud of the *sacrifices* her parents made for the war effort. But she missed having breakfast with her mother. She missed her father, too.

"You look sad," said Robert. He had a mouthful of *cereal* and milk *dribbling* from his *chin*. "What's wrong?"

爱丽丝和罗伯特来到厨房的时候,妈妈已经去上班了。自从爸爸去了欧洲战场,妈妈就在一家生产轮船配件的工厂上班。和许多女人一样,爱丽丝的妈妈做起了曾经是男人们从事的工作。美国需要新的船只来打赢这场战争,女人们只好一周工作6天-7天,每天8个-12个小时,这样才能保证工厂不停业。

爱丽丝以父母为战争做出的牺牲感到骄傲。但是她怀念与妈妈共进早餐的日子。她也十分想念爸爸。

"你不开心,"罗伯特问道。嘴里塞满了麦片粥,牛奶也流到了下巴上。"出什么事了吗?"

---

sacrifice *n.* 牺牲
dribble *v.* 一点一滴的落下;细流

cereal *n.* 由谷类制成的食品
chin *n.* 下巴

◆ ALICE'S BIRTHDAY CAKE

"Nothing," Alice lied as she *absently* wiped her brother's face with a *napkin*. Robert was right. Alice was feeling sad. Her thirteenth birthday was tomorrow. In the past, Alice looked forward to her birthdays, but this year was different. Her father usually would wake her up by *belting out* the song Happy Birthday to You. It always made her laugh. "Unlucky thirteen," Alice said to herself as she helped Robert tie his shoes.

Chapter Two

Since Alice's mother worked long hours at the factory, Alice did more *chores* around the house. Most days Alice did not mind the extra responsibility, she felt good being able to help out. Today the one chore she had to do— grocery shopping—made Alice want

---

"没事，"爱丽丝没有说实话，漫不经心地用餐巾纸将弟弟的脸擦干净。罗伯特说对了。爱丽丝的确很难过。明天就是她13岁的生日了，可是今年会有些不同。爸爸通常都会唱着"生日快乐"歌把她叫醒。这总会让爱丽丝很开心。"不吉利的13，"爱丽丝一边想着，一边帮弟弟系鞋带。

第二章

妈妈在工厂要工作很长时间，所以爱丽丝承担了很多家务。很多时候，爱丽丝都不会在意承担了额外的负担，相反，她为自己能出一份力而感到开心。今天，她只要完成一件家务——购物——这使爱丽丝想发牢

---

absently *adv.* 心不在焉地；茫然地
belt out 引吭高歌；高唱出
napkin *n.* 纸巾；餐巾纸
chore *n.* 杂务；杂活

GROWING PAINS I

to *groan* with the effort it would take. Alice was not in the mood to travel from store to store to find all the items on the shopping list her mother had left along with money and their *ration* book.

Each family had a ration book with stamps for certain kinds of food. Because of the war, the government rationed food to make sure there was enough for everyone when supplies were limited. Stores ran out of the most popular items, such as coffee and canned goods. Alice had to match the right stamps from her ration book with the food on her mother's list. Shopping could take a long time.

Alice saw milk on the list and was not looking forward to another *marathon* shopping trip. Milk could be difficult to find. Once there was no milk, so they had to eat their cereal with water instead.

骚。她真的没有心情，拿着妈妈留下的钱和配给簿，挨家店地去挑选妈妈写在单子上的物品。

每家都有一本配给簿，不同图章代表不同的食物。因为是战时，政府实施食物配给以确保当供给受限时，人人都不会挨饿。像咖啡和罐装食物这样的大众商品，商店通常是没货的。爱丽丝必须把妈妈留下的购物单子和配给票对应起来。所以，购物可能要花费很长时间。

爱丽丝看到单子上有牛奶，而买到牛奶要走上好远的路，她一点也不想那样做。牛奶不是容易找到的商品。一旦没有牛奶了，他们只能用水代替牛奶冲麦片。

---

groan *v.* 抱怨；呻吟　　　　　　　　　　　ration *n.* 定量；配给量
marathon *adj.* 马拉松式的

◆ ALICE'S BIRTHDAY CAKE

Alice washed dishes before she and Robert left for school. Tomorrow was Alice's birthday, but she knew there wasn't going to be a party. Alice saw there were no ration stamps left for sugar, butter, or eggs. Her mother couldn't bake a cake with just flour. Alice and Robert walked to school in silence.

Right after school, Alice had to go grocery shopping. She waved bye to her friends as she *grabbed* Robert's hand. Her friends had been *whispering* and quickly stopped when they saw Alice. Alice wondered if they were talking about her. She hadn't told them it would be her birthday tomorrow. What was the use? No cake, no party, so no reason to tell her friends. Alice wondered if that's what they were whispering about. Maybe they knew it was her birthday,

爱丽丝把碗洗干净后，同罗伯特一起向学校走去。明天就是爱丽丝的生日了，可是，她知道不会有任何庆祝。爱丽丝清楚，糖、黄油和鸡蛋的配给票都已经用完了。只有面粉，妈妈是无法做蛋糕的。爱丽丝和罗伯特静静地走在上学的路上。

刚刚放学，爱丽丝就得去买家里需要的东西。她一边握住弟弟的手，一边和朋友挥手告别。她的朋友一直在窃窃私语，碰到她时又立刻停下来。爱丽丝想知道她们是否在谈论她。她根本就没告诉她们，明天是她的生日。有什么用呢？没有蛋糕，没有庆祝，所以没有理由告诉她们。爱丽

grab *v.* 抓取；抓住　　　　　　　　　　　　whisper *v.* 密谈；耳语

GROWING PAINS I

and they were *mad* they hadn't been invited to a party.

Alice walked to Main Street, her mood darker than the blackout curtains in her room. It took three stores before she found everything on the list. Robert had been quiet. He didn't even complain that the stores did not have his favorite canned *peaches*. She was thankful.

On the walk home, Alice and Robert passed an elderly *couple* sitting on their front *porch*. Alice saw a blue star in their window. A blue star meant that a man from that family was a soldier away at war. A gold star meant that the soldier had been killed. Alice and Robert passed many blue stars. Alice thought of the blue star in their window at home and wished that her father was home safe.

丝想，这可能就是她们在秘密讨论的事情吧。也许，她们知道明天是她的生日，正为她没邀请她们参加庆祝会而生气呢。

爱丽丝走在大街上，心情比房间里的窗帘还要灰暗。她走了三家商店，才把单子上的所有东西都买齐全了。罗伯特一直都很安静。他甚至没有抱怨商店里没有他最喜欢的桃罐头。爱丽丝心存感激。

回家的路上，姐弟俩经过一座房子，一对夫妇正坐在前门廊厅里。爱丽丝看到了他们窗上的一颗蓝色星星。蓝色的星星代表这家有一个男人已奔赴战场作战。金色的星星代表这家有人阵亡。爱丽丝想到了自己家里窗上的蓝色星星，她希望爸爸能平安回家。

---

mad *adj.* 很生气；气愤
couple *n.* 夫妇；对

peach *n.* 桃子；桃树
porch *n.* 门廊；走廊

◆ ALICE'S BIRTHDAY CAKE

Chapter Three

Alice's mother was always tired when she got home from work in the evening. Alice tried to have dinner ready so her mother could enjoy a bath before they sat down together to eat.

At dinner, Robert told them about how he and his friends had won the *scrap* drive. They had collected more bits of metal and tin *foil* than any other team. The metal was used to make *materials* for the war effort.

After dinner, Robert played with his toy soldiers as they all listened to the radio, hoping for good news about the war. "When is father coming home?" Robert asked.

第三章

每天晚上，妈妈下班回家后，总是一身疲惫。爱丽丝尽量把饭做好，这样就可以等妈妈洗过澡后，一起吃晚饭。

吃饭时，罗伯特讲述了他和朋友们是如何赢得捡金属废料的比赛。他们收集到的金属碎片和锡箔纸比任何队都多。这些金属废料可以用来生产战备品以支援战争。

晚饭过后，大家一起收听广播，希望听到有关战争的好消息。罗伯特一边玩着玩具士兵，一边问道，"爸爸什么时候回来呀？"

---

scrap *n.* 废料；碎屑　　　　　　　　　　　　foil *n.* 箔；金属箔
material *n.* 物资；原料

GROWING PAINS I

"Soon, dear," said Mother in a soft voice. Alice knew that her mother missed their father as much as she did. Alice would not complain about her day to her mother. She knew birthdays were small when compared to helping the war effort, but Alice, afraid her *disappointment* would show, went to bed early. Upstairs, she cried herself to sleep.

Chapter Four

To Alice's great surprise, she woke the next morning to the sound of singing. Her mother and brother were standing next to her bed, belting out *Happy Birthday to You* in their loudest voices just as her father would have. At first, Alice thought she was dreaming. But it was really happening.

"You didn't forget!" Alice said happily, sitting up in bed.

"很快，孩子，"母亲轻声细语地说道。爱丽丝知道妈妈和她们一样也十分想念爸爸。爱丽丝不会向妈妈抱怨。因为她知道，与支援战争相比，生日显得微不足道。但是爱丽丝担心自己会流露出失望的表情，就提前上床去睡觉。在楼上，她哭着睡着了。

第四章

让爱丽丝吃惊的是，第二天早上，她伴随着歌唱声醒来。妈妈和弟弟就站在床边，大声地唱着"祝你生日快乐"，就像爸爸那样高声唱着。起初，爱丽丝以为她在做梦，但这确实是真的。

"你们没有忘记！"爱丽丝高兴地说，在床上坐了起来。

---

disappointment *n.* 失望；沮丧

◆ ALICE'S BIRTHDAY CAKE

"Of course not," said her mother. She gave Alice a big birthday hug.

It was Saturday. Alice's mother did not have to work this weekend, so they all ate their cereal together. Alice was much happier that today was her thirteenth birthday. Her blackout curtains no longer *reflected* her mood.

After breakfast, Mother gave Alice some money so she and Robert could go to the movies. "It's a *double feature*," Alice's mother said. "Have fun!"

Alice and Robert walked to the movie theater. Alice would rather have had a party, but she was happy her mother and brother remembered she turned thirteen today. Alice looked for her friends in the line of people buying tickets, but they were not there. "That's

"当然没有，"妈妈说道。她给了爱丽丝一个大大的生日拥抱。

今天是星期六。这周妈妈不用去上班，所以她们坐在一起吃麦片粥。爱丽丝13岁的生日，她比往常都高兴。她的心情再也不因房间里的窗帘影响而暗淡了。

吃过早饭，妈妈给了姐弟俩一些钱，他们可以去看电影了。"是双片连映，"妈妈说道。"你们要玩得开心些！"

爱丽丝和罗伯特向电影院走去。虽然爱丽丝还是希望能有一个生日庆祝会，但是她已经非常开心，妈妈和弟弟记得她已经13岁了。爱丽丝在买票的队伍中寻找着她的朋友，可是谁也没发现。"太奇怪了，"她想。通

reflect v. 反映；反照   double feature 两片连映

GROWING PAINS I

strange," she said to herself. Usually her friends went to the movies on Saturdays. Alice wondered if they were having fun without her. If only I was having a birthday party, she thought sadly. She bought two tickets and *led* her brother inside.

Chapter Five

As they left the movie theater, Robert said, "Hurry, let's run home."

The bright sun hurt Alice's eyes after being so long in the dark theater. "What's the big rush?" said Alice. She had enjoyed the movie, but she still felt disappointed that she wasn't going to have a party. Alice knew they did not have the ration stamps for a cake, but a party would have been nice. Alice thought about looking for her friends, but then she *wondered* if they were still her friends after all.

常她的朋友们都会在周六来看电影。她想，是不是朋友们出去玩了而没有邀请她。要是有生日庆祝会该多好。她想起这事就感到难过。她买了两张票，带着弟弟进入影院。

第五章

当电影散场时，罗伯特说道，"快，我们跑着回家吧。"

从黑暗的影院里出来，外面的强光刺得爱丽丝眼睛不舒服。"为什么这么急呀？"爱丽丝问道。她很喜欢这电影，可是心里仍为没有生日庆祝会而感到失落。爱丽丝知道，家里已经没有蛋糕配给票了，但是有生日庆祝会总是好的。爱丽丝想找到她的朋友们，但她不确定她们是否还愿意和

---

lead *v.* 领（路）；带领　　　　　　　　wonder *v.* 想知道；想要弄明白

◆ ALICE'S BIRTHDAY CAKE

Robert had started to run home already, so Alice jogged to catch up to him.

Once home, Robert had left the front door hanging open. Alice walked in and closed the door behind her. The house seemed strangely silent. Where was Robert? Where was her mother? Alice felt scared. The door to the dining room was closed. Alice started to push it open. "Hello! Anybody here?" she called out in a *curious* voice.

"Surprise!"

Alice slowly *blinked* her eyes as if what she saw would disappear. All her friends were standing around the dining table. On the table was a big cake with pink frosting. Alice's friends sang Happy Birthday to You.

"But... how... I didn't think..." Alice could *barely* speak, she was so

---

她做朋友。罗伯特已经开始朝家里跑去，爱丽丝也跑了起来去追上他。

跑回家，罗伯特让门敞开着。爱丽丝走了进去，并随手把门关上。房子里异常安静。罗伯特去了哪里？妈妈在干什么呢？爱丽丝感到不安。餐厅的门关着。爱丽丝便推开门。"有人在吗？"爱丽丝好奇地喊道。

"惊喜！"

爱丽丝慢慢地眨着眼睛，生怕眼前的一切会消失。她的朋友们正站在桌子四周。而桌上摆放着一个用粉色糖霜装饰的大蛋糕。爱丽丝的朋友们为她唱起生日快乐歌。

"但是……我真的没想到……"爱丽丝几乎说不出话来，她太高兴

---

curious　adj. 好奇的；有求知欲的
barely　adv. 勉强；几乎不

blink　v. 眨眼睛

GROWING PAINS I

happy.

"I saved our ration stamps so I could buy enough butter, eggs, and sugar for your cake," explained Alice's mother. "Your friends' families helped, too."

"We thought you might have guessed what all the whispering was about," said Alice's friend Elizabeth. "We were talking about which stamps we still needed for your cake."

Alice saw a letter next to the cake. "What's this?" she asked her mother.

"Read it," her mother *suggested*.

Alice read the letter. It was a birthday card from her father. He was safe. Alice was wrong when she thought that turning thirteen was unlucky. She felt awful for thinking everyone had forgotten about her. All her friends and family loved her very much and had made turning thirteen truly special.

3。
　　"我攒下了我们的黄油、鸡蛋和白糖的配给票，这样就可以为你做蛋糕了，"妈妈解释道。"你朋友的家人也帮了大忙。"
　　"我们想你可能猜到了我们在小声地说着什么，"爱丽丝的朋友伊丽莎白说道。"我们在商量，你的生日蛋糕还需要什么配给票。"
　　爱丽丝看到了蛋糕旁边的一封信。"这是什么？"她问妈妈。
　　"那就看看吧，"妈妈建议道。
　　爱丽丝看了信，是爸爸寄来的生日卡片。他一切安好。当初爱丽丝认为13岁生日是不幸运的，她想错了。她真不该认为大家忘记了她的生日……她的朋友和家人都非常爱她，他们使13变得非常特殊。

---

suggest *v.* 建议；提议

11

Mirroring Miranda

Chapter 1

Miranda James looked long and hard at the 12-year-old girl in the mirror. "This is the summer you are going to do it, girl!" she said aloud. "You are going to write a science *fiction* story that will get published, and win the Hugo Award or the Nebula Award or maybe even both."

Isaac Asimov, Ray Bradbury, Robert Heinlein, Ursula Le Guin and all the great sci-fi, or SF writers won these *prestigious* science fiction

---

镜子中的米兰达

第一章

米兰达·詹姆斯使劲儿地看着镜子里的12岁女孩，看了很长时间。"这个暑假你就要成为这个样子，小丫头！"她大声说道。"你要写一篇科幻小说，要发表，还要获得'雨果奖'或者'星云奖'，要不就两个都拿。"

艾萨克·阿西莫夫、雷·布莱德伯里、罗伯特·海因莱因、厄休拉·勒吉恩，所有伟大的科幻作家都获得过科幻界的这两项大奖。这些人和其

---

fiction n. 小说；虚构的事   prestigious adj. 有名望的；享有声望的

awards. These, and other famous SF authors, were on Miranda's *alphabetized*, must-read list. Then she penciled-in her own name: James, between Heinlein and Le Guin. Thinking about her future fame sent a cold *shiver* up her *spine*.

Her award-winning story would become a bestseller, no doubt, then get turned into a *blockbuster* movie starring... oh well, Miranda had lots of time to figure out that part. First, she had to write the story.

他的著名科幻作家一样，名字都出现在米兰达的必读书目上，并按姓氏进行了排序。接下来，米兰达用铅笔把她自己的姓"詹姆斯"加到了"海因莱因"和"勒吉恩"之间。（译者注：在英文中，"詹姆斯"首字母为"J"，位于"海因莱因"(H)和"勒吉恩"(L)之间。）想到自己未来有这么高的声望，她不禁感到一阵寒战。

她的获奖作品将成为畅销书，然后无疑会被改编成一部非常卖座的电影，主角就选……哦，好吧，米兰达幻想未来已经花了太多时间。她还是需要先写出故事来。

---

alphabetize *v.* 按字母顺序排列
spine *n.* 脊柱；脊椎

shiver *v.* 哆嗦；颤抖
blockbuster *n.* 极成功的电影

◆ MIRRORING MIRANDA

This would not be Miranda's first science fiction story. She wrote seventeen other science fiction stories and *submitted* every one of them to her favorite sci-fi magazine, *Future Tense*. So what if she received seventeen rejection letters? With each letter she received an encouraging note back from the editor.

"Dear Sir/Madam: Thank you for your submission. However, it does not meet our publishing needs at this time. Good luck with your future *endeavors*."

Miranda didn't care that they were rejection letters. The editor had said "good"! Strangely, when Miranda read the letter aloud and reached the word "good," she *faintly* heard it *echo* from her bedroom

---

这并不是米兰达的科幻小说处女作。她已经写过17部科幻小说，并且都投稿给她最喜欢的科幻杂志——《将来时》。可是如果她收到17封退稿信要怎么办呢？在收到的每一封退稿信中，都有编辑写给她的鼓励的言语。

"亲爱的先生/女士：谢谢您的来稿。但是，目前您的投稿还不符合我社的出版标准。请继续努力，祝您好运。"

米兰达并不在乎这些来信是退稿信。编辑说了"好！"奇怪的是，每当米兰达大声读信时，读到"好"字时，她就好像听到她卧室的镜子里发出了回音，或者至少她觉得她听到了。不管怎样，她都把这种回音当作一

---

submit *v.* 呈送；提出　　　　　　endeavor *n.* 努力；尽力
faintly *adv.* 虚弱地；微弱地　　　echo *v.* 发出回声；产生回想

GROWING PAINS I

mirror. Or at least she thought she heard it. Either way, she took it as an encouraging sign and *vowed* to eat, sleep, breathe, and, most importantly, read science fiction all through the summer.

Although the list she had made of sci-fi authors was in alphabetical order, Miranda decided to read the authors in a random order. Randomness felt more like science fiction to her. As it turned out, she ended up reading a different number of books by each author by the end of the summer. In fact, Miranda had read two books by C. J. Cherryh and had learned a lot about Ms. Cherryh's sci-fi style.

Chapter 2

"What are you doing in your room on this beautiful day?" asked

---

种鼓励的标志,并且发誓这个暑假要在科幻的世界里吃饭、睡觉、呼吸,最重要的是,要坚持读科幻小说。

尽管在书单上,米兰达是按科幻作家们的姓氏顺序排列的,但她还是决定不按照固定的顺序来阅读这些书目。在她看来,以任意的顺序来读更有科幻的感觉。结果,到了暑假结束,她把每位作家的书都读了一些。事实上,米兰达已经读完了两本C.J.雀芮的书,并且了解了雀芮女士的科幻风格。

第二章

"这么好的天,你在屋里干什么呢?"她的哥哥哈里斯问道。哈里斯

VOW *v.* 发誓;郑重宣告

◆ MIRRORING MIRANDA

her brother Harris, a senior in high school. "I hope you're not talking to yourself again."

"Maybe I am, and then again maybe the voice you heard was an *android* in the fourth *dimension* controlling your mind," said Miranda. She had just started reading a book about androids—robots that look like humans. The day before, she finished a book set in the fourth dimension, which meant time was constantly shifting in a mind-freaky way. Next, she planned to read a book about an evil scientist who invents a ray gun that *zombifies* people so that he can take over the world.

"I'm taking the dog to the park to play fetch. Want to come?" asked Harris.

现在读高中。他说:"希望你不是又在自言自语。"

"可能是吧,你再听到的声音还有可能是来自控制你思想的四维空间来的机器人的声音呢,"米兰达说。她现在刚开始读一本关于机器人的书,是那种看起来很像人类的机器人。而前一天,她刚读完一本有关四维空间的书,讲的是时间是一直在变化中的,而这种变化会让人发狂。接下来,她准备读的书是讲一位很邪恶的科学家发明了一把光线枪,这把枪能够使人类失去思维能力,这样他就可以统治全世界。

"我要带小狗去公园玩抛物游戏。你来不来?"哈里斯问道。

---

android *n.* 机器人　　　　　　　　　　dimension *n.* 维;尺寸
zombify *v.* 使呆板;使木讷

GROWING PAINS I

"You go. I have work to do," Miranda replied.

"Not another one of your ridiculous stories!" exclaimed Harris.

"They are not ridiculous! They are what we science fiction writers call 'cautionary tales'."

"Well, I hope it is better than the one about the *mutant* broccoli that grew so big it *squished* Milwaukee," teased Harris.

"It was a *zucchini*, for your information, and it was Cincinnati that got squashed! Don't you get it? Zucchini is a type of a squash. That is what we writers call a play on words. And because the greedy agribusiness *overlords* were using illegal fertilizer that accidentally

---

"你去吧。我还有事，"米兰达回答说。

"别告诉我你又有了一个荒唐的故事！"哈里斯嚷道。

"我的故事才不荒唐呢！我们科幻小说作家都把它们叫作'警示性故事'。"

"好，我希望你这个故事比那个基因突变的甘蓝长到特别大然后把密尔沃基压扁的故事好看点，"哈里斯取笑她说。

"你弄清楚，那是西葫芦，而且压扁的是辛辛那提！你到底懂不懂？西葫芦是美国南瓜的一种。（译者注：英文中，squash一词兼有"压扁"和"美国南瓜"的意思，所以米兰达说这是"文字游戏"。）这不过我们

---

mutant *adj.* 基因突变的；变异的
zucchini *n.* 西葫芦

squish *v.* 压扁；压烂
overlord *n.* 霸主；大君主

◆ MIRRORING MIRANDA

gets *zapped* with radioactive waste dumped on it by the *corrupt* politicians who ran the nuclear power plant, the zucchini grows so big it squashes them all. Tit-for-tat. We sci-fi writers call this an *allegory*."

"Well," spouted Harris, "if you feel like exercising something besides your *overactive* imagination, let me know. We nonwriters call this an invitation."

That Harris made her so mad! He told her to leave science fiction to boys; she should write stories about lost kittens, pink princesses,

---

作家玩的文字游戏罢了。而且那是因为贪婪的农业大亨们使用的非法肥料意外出错，因为运行核电站的腐败政客们在肥料上扔了放射性垃圾，然后西葫芦才长得太大把那些都压扁了的。这叫'一报还一报'。我们科幻作家把这叫作'寓言'。"

"好，"哈里斯也开始滔滔不绝起来，"如果您除了练习超级活跃的想象力之外还想做些其他的运动，就告诉我。我们非作家把这叫作'邀请'。"

这个哈里斯简直要让她发疯了！哈里斯告诉她，写科幻是男孩子的事；她应该写写迷路的小猫、可爱的公主和野马之间发生的故事。米兰达

---

zap *v.* 杀死，摧毁
allegory *n.* 寓言

corrupt *adj.* 腐败的；堕落的
overactive *adj.* 过于活跃的；活跃得不正常的

GROWING PAINS I

and wild horses. Miranda knew some girls who liked that romantic stuff, but it made her want to throw up. Still, Harris was right about getting exercise, so she *reluctantly* put aside her writing and rode her bike to the library. She checked out an odd number of books by Ursula K. Le Guin—"a *female* sci-fi writer, thank you!" she said aloud to Harris, though Harris wasn't anywhere around.

Miranda looked at her list of authors and now planned to read more books by female sci-fi writers. Plus, she figured that an odd number would be a good idea because odd was sort of *weird*, and she felt a weird story *brewing* inside of her.

知道有些女生很喜欢这些浪漫的东西，但她一想就觉得恶心。但是，哈里斯关于运动的建议是有道理的，所以她很不情愿地把写作暂时搁下，骑车去了图书馆。她在图书馆查了几本（数量上她选择奇数）厄休拉·K·勒吉恩的书——"勒吉恩是位女科幻作家，谢谢！"她对哈里斯大声说，尽管哈里斯根本没在她身边。

米兰达看着自己的作家名单，开始打算多读一些女科幻作家的作品。另外，她发现选择奇数是很棒的做法，因为"奇数"与"奇怪"意思相近，（译者注：英文中，odd一词兼有"奇数"和"奇怪的"的意思，所以米兰达觉得选择奇数会有种怪异感。）她感觉自己心里也有一个奇怪的故事正在酝酿着。

---

reluctantly *adv.* 不愿意地；勉强地
weird *adj.* 怪异的；超自然的

female *adj.* 女性的；雌性的
brew *v.* 酝酿；筹划

◆ MIRRORING MIRANDA

Chapter 3

Dozens of tales *rambled* around James Miranda's brain, waiting to be put on paper. But the guys in her class laughed at him whenever she told them her stories about *knights* in shining *armor* saving *damsels* in distress. "No wonder," said her big sister. "That's girl stuff." But James' adventures also had wizards and trolls and fire-breathing dragons, she explained.

Her sister didn't listen. She told her to get a life. Because if she had a life, she'd not only have fun, her'd have something real to write about.

James had plenty of fun writing her stories, thank you very much. One day, she'd be famous because of them, too. So she just kept

---

第三章

在米兰达·詹姆斯的头脑里已经有几十个故事跳来跳去，就等她付诸笔端。但是只要她讲起穿着闪亮盔甲的骑士救出了受困的小女孩，她班上的男生们就取笑他。"一点也不奇怪，"她的大姐说，"那是女孩们喜欢的故事。"她解释说，但是詹姆斯的历险中也有男巫、巨怪和喷火龙。

她姐姐不听她说什么，只是告诉她要过有意义的生活。因为如果她过有意义的生活，就不会只找一些乐子，而是会写出更真实的东西。

谢谢，詹姆斯从现在写的故事中就得到了很多乐趣。总有一天，她会因为这些故事而成名。所以她只要跟着感觉继续写就对了。"这些都是好

---

ramble *v.* 蔓生；蔓延　　　　knight *n.* 爵士；骑士
armor *n.* 盔甲；装甲　　　　　damsel *n.* 少女；姑娘

GROWING PAINS I

writing what she felt she had to write. "They are good stories," she heard the voice inside her say.

And then she would say aloud: "Good."

Reading all these science fiction books is definitely helping my writing, Miranda thought. So far, she especially enjoyed the space-travel books by Arthur C. Clarke. Too bad she had not read him first.

Clarke's books were considered "pure" science fiction. They were made-up stories, but based on *scientific* truths. His books looked at how real scientific discoveries could put people in *situations* where they had to make decisions that could change people's lives for the better — or worse.

故事，"她听到自己心中的声音说。

然后她就会大声说："好。"

米兰达想，读这些科幻故事肯定会帮助我更好地写作。读了这么多，她最喜欢的就是亚瑟·C·克拉克的有关太空旅行的书。遗憾的是她没有最先读克拉克的书。

克拉克的书被认为是"纯"科幻。虽然故事是虚构的，但是都是基于科学真理的基础之上。他的书讲的都是在各种情境中，人们应当如何利用真实的科学发现做出决定，而这些决定可以使人们的生活更加美好，或更加糟糕。

---

scientific *adj.* 科学的；系统的   situation *n.* 情况；处境

◆ MIRRORING MIRANDA

"Heavy stuff," said Miranda aloud. Then she felt another *chill* come over her. At first she thought it came from her realization that in the best sci-fi, mastering science often meant power over nature—just not human nature. But it was not a *tingly* feeling she was feeling, it was an icy *blast*, as if she was standing in front of an air conditioner that had just turned on. Once again she was in front of the mirror in her room, her hot, air-conditioner-less, fan-less room.

Feeling *creeped* out, she reached out to touch the mirror. It was cold to her touch, colder than an ice cube, almost as cold as frozen carbon dioxide gas, which she had been researching to use in a

---

"太沉重了，"米兰达大声说。紧接着她又感觉到一阵寒战。原来，她以前的知识使她觉得，最好的科幻小说里，懂得科学常常意味着拥有控制自然的力量——但是控制不了人类的本性。可是此刻的感觉不仅仅是种激动的感觉，而是一种冰冷感，仿佛她正站在刚刚打开的空调前面。而她其实是又一次站在自己房间的镜子前，屋里闷热，既没有空调，也没有风扇。

她蹑手蹑脚地走过去，伸手去摸镜子。摸到后她感觉一阵冰凉，镜子比冰块还凉，就像冰冻了的二氧化碳气体，这是她打算用在一本小说里的说法。她用食指碰到镜子的那一刻，食指麻木了。如果不是她退缩了，米

---

chill *n.* 寒意；害怕的感觉
blast *n.* 冲击波；一阵
tingly *adj.* 感到兴奋的；引起激动的
creep *v.* 悄悄地缓慢行进；蹑手蹑脚地移动

GROWING PAINS I

story. When she touched the mirror with her index finger, it turned *numb*. If she hadn't inched, Miranda was sure her finger would have stuck to the mirror!

Then Miranda tried a different experiment. She breathed on the mirror. It fogged up. That reminded Miranda of when she was younger, and would breathe onto the cold car window in winter. When it fogged up, which she now knew was caused by *condensation*, she'd write her name on the window, then watch the letters disappear as the fog *evaporated*. The cool part was that the letters in her name would reappear magically if she blew another warm breath on the same spot. Now she knew it wasn't magic that caused this, it was science.

What was strange now, however, was that this wasn't winter,

兰达确定她的手指肯定会粘在镜子上的！

　　接着米兰达又做了一个不同的试验。她哈气到镜子上，那口气就成了雾状。这使米兰达想起了她小时候，冬天向寒冷的车窗哈气的情形。她知道起雾是因为空气凝结形成的，她会在起雾的车窗上写自己的名字，雾气蒸发时再看着那些字母一个个消失不见。最神奇的是，如果她在同样的地方再哈一口气，那些字母又会像变魔术似的重现。现在她明白这一切并不是魔术，而是科学。

　　而此刻最奇怪的是，现在既不是冬天，面前也不是车窗，而且当镜

numb *adj.* 麻木的；发愣的　　　　　　condensation *n.* 凝结；冷凝
evaporate *v.* 蒸发；消失

there wasn't a car window, and when the fog evaporated from the mirror, Miranda could read her name as she had written it on her alphabetized reading list: James Miranda—last name first. But, she had not written her name that way on the mirror... she shivered again.

Chapter 4

Had Miranda written her name that way on the mirror a long time ago? To take her mind off this *creepy* feeling, Miranda picked up a book by Roger Zelazny. He was the fourth sci-fi author she would

---

子上的雾气散去的时候，米兰达还能看见她之前写下的名字，就像她在那张书单上写下的名字一样：詹姆斯·米兰达——姓在名的前面。（译者注：英语国家人的姓名顺序通常为：名在前，姓在后。如"米兰达·詹姆斯"，"米兰达"是名，"詹姆斯"是姓。）但是，她在镜子上写名字的时候并没有把姓写在前面……她又打了个冷战。

第四章

米兰达是很久以前在镜子上这样写过自己的名字么？为了躲开这种怪异感觉的困扰，米兰达拿起了一本罗杰·泽拉兹尼的书。他是米兰达计划在暑期阅读的第四位科幻作家。米兰达仔细地看着封面上的作者照片。

---

creepy *adj.* 令人毛骨悚然的

GROWING PAINS I

read that summer. She studied his picture on the book *jacket*. The biographical notes said he died a few years ago, and often wrote about magic and fantasy worlds.

Miranda read late into the night. Her eyes *burned*, but she couldn't stop. She had to find out what happened to Zelazny's famous character, Prince Corwin of Amber.

Sometime around midnight, Miranda *dozed* off. She dreamed that a dark-haired boy in a *tuxedo* spoke to her from the mirror.

"You can do it," he said. "Just keep writing."

Miranda woke up in a cold sweat. "Bong, bong," struck the grandfather clock in the dining room. "Two o'clock in the morning

---

传记中说他已经在几年前去世了。他的故事通常发生在魔幻、奇妙的世界里。

　　米兰达那天晚上读书读到很晚。她的眼睛很痛，但她就是停不下来。她想要知道泽拉兹尼笔下著名的主人公——安珀的柯温王子——到底是什么样的结局。

　　大概是半夜的时候，米兰达打起瞌睡来。她梦见穿着无尾礼服的黑发男孩从镜子里对她讲话。

　　"你可以的，"他说，"要坚持写下去。"

　　米兰达醒来时感到一阵冷汗。"梆，梆，"餐厅里的古董钟敲了两

---

jacket *n.* 封面；护封　　　　　　　burn *v.* 刺痛；使有火辣感
doze *v.* 瞌睡；假寐　　　　　　　tuxedo *n.* 无尾礼服

would be a good time for something *spooky* to happen in one of my stories," Miranda said to herself as she reached for her journal to make some late-night notes. As she gazed at the mirror, another icy blast swooshed past her, and she froze momentarily. All of a sudden a face peered at her from what seemed like inside the mirror. "Oh my gosh! You're... Zelazny Roger!" she cried.

Chapter 5

Prince Saffron *sheathed* his sword and raised his shield. "Onward, Valiant," he commanded, and his enormous, white steed took off at full *gallop*. Acitcratna, the ice-breathing dragon, had turned the prince into an ice sculpture.

下。"凌晨两点是个写怪异故事的好时间，这可以成为我的一个故事，"米兰达自言自语着去拿她的笔记本，记下她深夜里的一些念头。她盯着镜子的时候，又打了一个冷战，有一瞬间她僵在了那里。那一刻，在镜子里仿佛有一张脸看着她。"哦，天哪！你是……罗杰·泽拉兹尼！"她大喊道。

第五章

萨伏龙王子放剑入鞘，拿起盾牌。"前进，勇士，"他命令道。于是，他那高大的白色骏马就全速飞奔起来。萨西克瑞特娜，一条会吐冰的飞龙把这位王子变成了一座冰制的雕塑。

---

spooky *adj.* 怪异吓人的；阴森恐怖的　　　　sheathe *v.* 把……插入鞘中
gallop *n.* 飞奔；疾驰

GROWING PAINS I

"I'm not Zelazny Roger," said the voice in the mirror. "But I, too, am a *magnificent* writer, and if you'll excuse me, I have to go save a princess."

Was Miranda still dreaming? "Ow!" she cried as she *pinched* herself. *Nope*, she was awake. Or was she in a *nightmare* in which she was dreaming she was awake?

Hadn't she read a story where something like that happened? She checked her notes. It could have been one of the books by Octavia Butler, who was the third author she had read . . . Or could it have been one of the five books she read by the previous author?

Maybe Harris was correct about her need to take a break from

"我不是罗杰·泽拉兹尼，"镜子里的声音说道，"但我也是一位杰出的作家。请允许我失陪一下，我要去救一位公主。"

米兰达还在梦中吗？"哎哟！"她掐了自己一下，疼得叫了起来。她醒着呢，没有做梦。还是她在噩梦中，梦见自己醒了？

她有没有读过类似于这样的故事呢？她翻看着自己的笔记。可能是奥克塔维亚·布特勒的作品之一，这是她读的第三位作家……或者是她之前读的那位作家的五本书之一？

也许哈里斯说的对，她应该从科幻的世界里出来放松一下了。突然她

---

magnificent *adj.* 出色的；了不起的
nope *adv.* 不是；没有

pinch *v.* 捏；掐；拧
nightmare *n.* 噩梦；噩梦般的经历

◆ **MIRRORING MIRANDA**

sci-fi. Then she realized what must be happening.

"All right, Harris," she said. "I know you are playing a trick on me. Ha-ha, you got me. You can come out now."

"My name isn't Harris," said the face in the mirror. "It is Miranda. James Miranda."

"James . . . Miranda? That's my name, too, but *backward*," said Miranda. "I'm Miranda James."

"I know," said the face in the mirror. The face belonged to a boy that seemed to be about 12 years old. In fact, the face looked like Miranda's— if she had been a boy.

就明白了这一切是怎么回事，一定是的。

"好吧，哈里斯，"她说，"我知道是你在搞恶作剧。哈哈，你已经吓到我了。现在你可以出来了。"

"我不叫哈里斯，"镜子中的面孔说道，"我叫米兰达。詹姆斯·米兰达。"

"詹姆斯……米兰达？那也是我的名字，但是我的是反过来的，"米兰达说，"我叫米兰达·詹姆斯。"

"我知道，"镜子中的面孔说道。这张脸看起来像是一个12岁男孩的脸。事实上，这张脸和米兰达很像——如果米兰达是男孩的话。

---

backward *adv.* 反向地；倒着地

GROWING PAINS I

"I've been trying to reach you," said James. "I sent you a message on the mirror, but my first attempt wasn't strong enough. Only my... our name made it through."

"James Miranda! On the mirror! So I wasn't making it up. It really happened."

"It is still happening," James said.

"Whoa! This is *freaky*. And *awesome*, just like a real science fiction story! You are me but in some *bizarre* parallel universe where things are backward or inside-out or..."

"Spirit twins is what we call them in my world," explained James.

"我一直在努力接近你,"詹姆斯说。"我通过镜子给你信息,但是我最初的尝试不够有力。只有我的……应该是我们的名字才可以做到。"

"詹姆斯·米兰达!在镜子里!所以这不是我编的。这一切都是真的。"

"而且还在继续,"詹姆斯说。

"哇哦!这太怪异了。而且太棒了,这就是个真实的科幻故事!你就是我,但你又是来自于某个奇异的平行星球,你们的星球与我们的正好相反,或者叫颠倒,或者叫……"

"在我的世界里,我们把这叫作'精神双胞胎',"詹姆斯解释道,

---

freaky *adj.* 很怪异的;罕见的 　　awesome *adj.* (口)出色的;棒极了的
bizarre *adj.* 意想不到的;异乎寻常的

MIRRORING MIRANDA

"Only a *select* few have them, which means that this is a rare gift." Then he explained about brain waves *intersecting* in a black hole in outer space, and why he had chosen to make himself known to Miranda, and how it would give him an actual true-life story of adventure to write.

Miranda was *enraptured* and took down everything James said. This was something no one was going to believe so she made sure she captured every word.

Epilogue

Miranda managed to capture the details of her talk with James

---

"只有极少数人才有这样的双胞胎,这确实是非常珍贵的礼物。"然后他又解释了脑波是如何在外太空的黑洞相互交织的,以及他为什么要让米兰达知道他的存在,还有这将成为他要书写的一个完全真实的故事。

米兰达喜不自胜,把詹姆斯说的都记了下来。因为这些事情说出去没有人会相信,所以她要确保一个字都没有漏掉。

尾声

米兰达努力地在日记里记录着她和詹姆斯谈话的每一个细节。这部日

---

select *adj.* 精选的
enraptured *adj.* 狂喜的;高兴过度的

intersect *v.* 相交;交叉
epilogue *n.* 结语;尾声

GROWING PAINS I

in her journal. And the journal became a book. She claims the part about freezing time *molecules* in carbon dioxide crystals to make a *portal* to the mirror world was the only part she made up. But that wasn't the main reason her first book, Pen Pal in the Looking Glass, became a bestseller. It was the way Miranda was able to *blend* science with fiction, so that the reader was never sure where the science ended and the fiction began, and vice-versa.

This is what keeps her fans coming back for more. Look for other sci-fi books by Miranda James in your local library. They are *guaranteed* to be a creepy read!

记成了一本书。她自己说，只有"用二氧化碳晶体冷冻时间分子来制造通向镜子的通道"这一部分是虚构的。但是这并不是她的第一本书——《镜子中的笔友》——成为畅销书的主要原因。主要原因是米兰达能够将科学与幻想相互融合，使读者无法分清哪部分是科学，哪部分是幻想。

她的书迷们也正是因为这个原因越来越喜欢读她的作品。到当地的图书馆去找一找米兰达·詹姆斯的科幻小说吧。读起来保证让你毛骨悚然！

---

molecule *n.* 分子；微粒
blend *v.* 使混合；掺和

portal *n.* 大门；入口
guarantee *v.* 担保；保证

12

The Mystery Twin

The Note

One dark and *blustery* night, Theresa Alto was *securing* the windows against a storm when she heard a rapid banging on the door. At first she *assumed* it was just the wind, but then it came again. She cautiously opened the door, keeping the chain fastened, for the Altos weren't expecting any visitors on a night like this. It was Mrs. Banks from the private *adoption* agency.

神秘的双胞胎

一张纸条

　　一个漆黑的夜晚，狂风大作。当特瑞莎·奥托正顶着风关窗户时，"咚咚咚"急促的敲门声响了起来。起初她以为只是风弄出的响声，可咚咚咚的声音又响起来。在这样的夜晚，奥托一家人不会有什么来访的客人，所以特瑞莎小心翼翼地打开门，门上的链条仍是拴着的。站在门外的是私人收养所的班克斯夫人。

---

blustery *adj.* 大风的；狂暴的
assume *v.* 臆断；想当然地认为
secure *v.* 把（某物）弄牢固
adoption *n.* 收养；领养

GROWING PAINS I

"I'm so sorry to disturb you on such a night," said Mrs. Banks. "But the *agency* is moving. When we moved a file *cabinet*, a note and photograph fell from behind it. It's about Heather. I thought you'd want to see it right away."

Thirteen years ago, Brad and Theresa Alto had adopted a beautiful baby girl. They had named her Heather after Theresa's favorite flower. Theresa placed her arm around Brad's, worried about what the note might say.

Mrs. Banks continued, "The note explains that the baby you adopted is a twin. The birth mother thought there might be a better

---

"很抱歉，这么糟的天气还来打扰你，"班克斯夫人说。"但是，收养所正在搬家，当我们移开一个档案柜的时候，一张纸条和一张照片从后面掉了出来，是关于希瑟的。我想你会想要马上看到它。"

13年前，布莱德和特瑞莎·奥托领养了一个漂亮的女婴。他们用特瑞莎最喜欢的石南花为她命名。（译者注：英文中希瑟(Heather)一词有石南花的意思。）特瑞莎用胳膊搂紧布莱德，不知道纸条上会写些什么。

班克斯夫人继续说："纸条上说你们领养的婴儿是一对双胞胎中的一个。亲生母亲认为婴儿分开将会得到更好的领养机会。在孩子父亲车祸去

---

agency *n.* 提供专项服务的机构   cabinet *n.* 橱柜

chance for the babies to be adopted if they were separated. She had to make a difficult decision after the car accident that killed the babies' father. She also included a photograph of the two of them in happier times. I thought it would be *comforting* for you to have the photograph, and exciting for Heather to know that she has a twin."

Telling Heather

After Mrs. Banks left, the Altos called Heather into the dining room and sat her down. As they ate dessert, Mrs. Alto started telling the story of Heather's adoption.

Heather *interrupted*, "You know I am really glad you are my

世后，她必须做出这个非常艰难的决定。她还留下一张两个孩子在一起时的照片，看起来很幸福。我想这张照片会让你们感到安慰，也能让希瑟知道自己有一个孪生同胞而感到兴奋。"

通知希瑟

班克斯夫人走后，奥托夫妇把希瑟叫到餐厅。他们一边吃着甜点，一边听奥托夫人讲述领养希瑟的故事。

希瑟打断说："你们知道吗，我非常高兴你们是我的父母，但我真的

---

comforting *adj.* 安慰的；令人欣慰的   interrupt *v.* 打断；打扰

GROWING PAINS I

parents, but really, do I have to hear this story all the time? I could *recite* it by heart!"

Mrs. Alto gazed lovingly at her thirteen-year-old daughter and *sighed*, and then glanced quickly at her husband. "I know, dear, but now that you're thirteen and such a grown-up young lady, there's something else we need to tell you. We didn't tell you before, because we just found out."

"What is it? Is something wrong?" asked Heather.

Her parents exchanged cautious looks, and then Mr. Alto began, "Dear, we love you very much."

"Yes, and... ?" said Heather, growing more and more impatient.

要一直听这种故事么？我已经背得滚瓜烂熟了！"

奥托夫人一边爱怜地注视着自己13岁的女儿，一边叹气，然后瞥了一眼丈夫，又对希瑟说："我知道，亲爱的。可现在你已经13岁了，有些事我们应该告诉你了。我们没有早点告诉你是因为我们也刚刚知道。"

"什么事？出什么事了么？"希瑟问道。

她的父母小心地对视了一下，然后奥托先生说："亲爱的，我们非常爱你。"

"是的，然后呢？"希瑟越来越不耐烦。

"嗯……你有一个孪生同胞。"奥托先生说道。

---

recite *v.* 背诵；叙述 sigh *v.* 叹气；叹息

◆ THE MYSTERY TWIN

"Well, you have a twin," Mr. Alto stated.

Heather sat *stunned* for a moment. "Really, a twin? You mean, I'm not an only child? Oh, you know how much I've always wanted a sister. This is the best news ever! Where is she?"

"Well," Mrs. Alto began, "your birth mother was afraid that if she left one family with twins, they might *reject* one or both of you, so she thought it best to separate you. The adoption agency can't tell us where your twin is, but Mrs. Banks did leave us this photograph of your birth parents and a note."

Heather stared at the photograph. "Wow," she whispered,

希瑟坐在那儿愣了片刻。"真的吗，一个孪生同胞？你是说我不是独生女？啊，你知道我多想有一个姐妹么？这是迄今为止我听过最好的消息了！她在哪里？"

"嗯，"奥托夫人说："你的亲生母亲担心，如果把你们托付给同一个家庭，他们只会接受一个或两个都不收，所以她想最好还是把你们分开。收养所不肯告诉我们你的孪生同胞身在何方，但是班克斯夫人给了我们这张你亲生父母的照片和一张纸条。"

希瑟凝视着这张照片。"哇！"她低声惊讶道："我有点像他们，是

---

stunned *adj.* 惊呆的   reject *v.* 拒绝

GROWING PAINS I

dumbfounded, "I kind of look like them, don't I? I guess I understand why they thought they had to separate us, but how will I ever know where my twin is? I'd hate to think I have a sister out there who I'll never know. Will you help me find her?"

"Of course, dear, we'll do everything we possibly can," Mrs. Alto *promised*. "But you know, your twin could be a brother as well as a sister."

"Oh, a brother, that would be okay too—just as long as it is a *sibling*!" exclaimed Heather.

"Why don't we place an ad in the paper?" Mr. Alto suggested. "Or maybe in a couple of papers, and some magazines, too."

"Great idea," agreed Mrs. Alto. "In the meantime, we should think

---

吗？我想我明白她为什么要将我们分开了，但是我怎样才能知道我的孪生妹妹在哪儿呢？一想到还有一个我无法相认的姐妹就觉得很遗憾。你们会帮我找到她吗？"

"当然，亲爱的，我们会尽力去找的，"奥托夫人许诺道，"但是，你的孪生同胞有可能是你的弟弟或者是妹妹。"

"哦，弟弟也好啊——只要是一个同胞就好！"希瑟大声说道。

"我们为什么不在报纸上登广告呢？"奥托先生建议道："或者是在几份报纸或一些杂志上也行。"

"好主意，"奥托夫人很赞成，"同时，我们应该想想要怎样判断那

---

dumbfounded *adj.* 惊呆的；惊讶的
sibling *n.* 兄弟；姊妹；同胞
promise *v.* 许诺；允诺

about how we're going to determine whether or not someone is *actually* related to Heather. Heather, why don't you come up with a list of things you think that you and a sibling might have in common."

Heather jumped up. "I'll get started right away. Thank you both so much!"

The Search

While Heather began to work on her list, Mr. and Mrs. Alto prepared an ad for several local and national newspapers and magazines. They were sure to include the exact date that Heather was born and a summary of the contents of the note that was left. The ad asked that anyone who could possibly be the missing twin to contact them immediately, and to send a photograph.

They waited and waited as *responses* began trickling in over

---

个人是不是真跟希瑟有关系。希瑟，你应该列出一些你觉得你和你的同胞应有的共同点。"

希瑟跳起来："我马上就开始列。太感谢爸爸妈妈了！"

搜寻

当希瑟开始拟写她的清单时，奥托夫妇正忙着在一些当地和全国的报纸及杂志上登广告。他们认真地将希瑟出生的确切日期和那张纸条内容的摘要登在了广告上。广告上请任何可能是希瑟同胞的人立刻联系他们，并随函附照片一张。

他们等待着。在接下来的几个星期中，他们陆陆续续地收到了回复。

---

actually *adv.* 实际上；事实上 　　　　　　　　　　response *n.* 响应；回答

the next few weeks. Most were just letters of support from people *describing* their own adoption and lost-sibling stories, but a few offered information that helped the Altos.

The Altos were finally able to narrow down the responses to three *candidates*, all of whom were the same age as Heather and had similar birth and adoption dates. All of them had come from the same adoption agency. The Altos contacted each of the families and set up interview times for the following week. Heather finished her list and got ready to finally meet her twin.

大多数回信只是表示支持，描述了自己的收养情况或与同胞失去联系的故事，但也有一小部分信息是对奥托一家人有帮助的。

　　奥托夫妇最终将所有回信范围缩小到三个人，他们的年龄都和希瑟相同，并且出生日期和收养日期也很接近。他们也都来自同一个领养机构。奥托夫妇联系了每一个家庭，并确定了下周见面的时间。希瑟也完成了她的清单，并期待着见到她的孪生同胞。

---

describe　*v.* 描述；描绘　　　　　　　　candidate　*n.* 应征者；候选人

◆ THE MYSTERY TWIN

The Interviews

Heather *apprehensively* reread her list while she waited for the first candidate to arrive. The list read:

Things about myself:

I have long, *curly* brown hair.

I have brown eyes.

I like to play chess.

见面

在等待第一位应征者到来时,希瑟担心地一遍又一遍地念着自己的清单。清单上写着:

关于我的事:

我有长长的棕色卷发。

我有棕色的眼睛。

我喜欢下象棋。

---

apprehensively *adv.* 担心地;忧虑地   curly *adj.* 卷曲的;卷毛的

GROWING PAINS I

I like cats better than dogs.
I love *peanut* butter.
I have attached *earlobes*.

Amelia skipped through the door. "I'm so excited you chose me to come see you, Heather! You know, I've always had the feeling that I had a sister, and when I read your ad, I almost fell out of my seat. I'm sure we're sisters, I can just sense it; I know you and I are twins!"

Amelia obviously wanted to be chosen as the missing twin. She gave very *elaborate* answers to Heather's questions, giving all the information she needed and more. The Altos were *wary*; they didn't

---

猫跟狗相比，我更喜欢猫。
我喜爱花生酱。
我没有耳垂。

阿米莉亚蹦蹦跳跳地走了进来，"希瑟，能有机会让我见到你，我真是太高兴了！你知道吗，我一直感觉我一定有个姐姐。当看到广告时，我激动的差点从椅子上跌下来。我很确定我们是姐妹，我能感觉得到；我就知道我们是双胞胎！"

显然，阿米莉亚是很想被确认为是那个失踪的双胞胎妹妹。对于希瑟的问题，她给了非常详尽细致的回答，甚至比希瑟所需要的信息还要多。

---

peanut *n.* 花生
elaborate *adj.* 详尽的；煞费苦心的
earlobe *n.* 耳垂
wary *adj.* 谨慎的；考虑周到的

want to think Heather's twin was the first candidate just because she was *energetic*. They wrote down Amelia's responses to Heather's questions.

Amelia:

She has long, straight brown hair with light *streaks* in it.

She says she has *hazel* eyes, but they look sort of brown.

She doesn't know how to play chess.

She likes cats, but she has a ferret and likes him better than either dogs or cats.

She's *allergic* to peanut butter, so she doesn't eat it.

Her earlobes are not attached.

奥托夫妇非常谨慎，他们不想仅仅因为她很有活力而把她当作希瑟的双胞胎妹妹。他们记录下了阿米莉亚对希瑟提问的回答。

阿米莉亚：

她有长长直直的棕色头发并有浅色发丝。

她说她有浅褐色的眼睛，但是看起来有点像棕色。

她不会下象棋。

她喜欢猫，但她最喜欢的是她那只白鼬，而不是猫狗。

她对花生酱过敏，所以不能吃。

她有耳垂。

---

energetic *adj.* 精力充沛的；有力的
hazel *adj.* 浅褐色的

streak *n.* 条纹；线条
allergic *adj.* 对……过敏的

GROWING PAINS I

The next to arrive was Harry, a thirteen-year-old boy with brown eyes and short, dark hair. Harry was soft-spoken and polite, and said he had read the ad in the local paper and lived just a few neighborhoods away. He answered all the questions very *concisely*, and seemed like a nice boy, just a little on the shy side, especially when compared to Amelia.

Harry:

He has short, curly, dark brown hair.

He has brown eyes.

He likes chess.

He doesn't like cats.

下一个进来的叫哈利，是一个13岁长着棕色眼睛和深色短发的男孩。哈利声音很温和而且很有礼貌，他说他看到了当地报纸上的广告，他家离这儿只有几个街区。他简洁地回答了所有的问题，看上去是一个不错的孩子，尤其是和阿米莉亚比起来，他显得有点害羞。

哈利：

他有深棕色的短卷发。

他有棕色的眼睛。

他喜欢下象棋。

他不喜欢猫。

---

concisely *adv.* 简明地；简洁地

◆ THE MYSTERY TWIN

Peanut butter is not his favorite food.

His earlobes are attached.

The final candidate was a very pleasant girl named Casey. She was also thirteen and had long, curly brown hair, brown eyes, and a nice smile. She *chatted* with the Altos, seeming very comfortable with the *entire* family. She even stayed for a while after the interview to talk about chess and school. After she left, the Altos listed her responses next to the others'.

Casey:

She has long, curly brown hair.

She has brown eyes.

She likes chess.

花生酱不是他最喜欢的食物。
他没有耳垂。
最后一个应征者是个非常讨人喜欢的女孩叫凯西。她也是13岁，有长长的棕色卷发、棕色眼睛和迷人的微笑。与奥托夫妇聊天的过程，使她看起来与整个家庭是那么融洽。她甚至在谈话结束后留下了来，聊了聊象棋和学校的事。她离开之后，奥托夫妇把她的回答和其他人的回答放在了一起。
凯西：
她有长长的棕色卷发。
她有棕色的眼睛。
她喜欢下象棋。

---

chat *v.* 闲谈；聊天   entire *adj.* 整个的；全体的

GROWING PAINS I

She likes cats.

She also likes peanut butter.

Her earlobes are not attached.

The Altos sat down and began comparing all the responses. They were a bit upset to find that none of the candidates were a perfect match, though all of them had enough in common that they might be related to Heather.

"I don't think we understand enough about *heredity* to *figure* out who is related and who is not," said Mr Alto.

"I agree", sighed Heather, who was terribly disappointed that they couldn't figure out who her twin was.

她喜欢猫。
她也喜欢花生酱。
她有耳垂。

奥托一家人坐在一起开始比较所有的应征者。让他们有些心烦的是，尽管他们都有一些跟希瑟相关的共同点，可没有一个应征者能完全匹配。

"我觉得我们不够了解遗传学，所以无法断定谁有关，谁无关。"奥托先生说。

"我同意，"希瑟叹息道。她因为找不出谁是她的孪生同胞而极度失望。

---

heredity *n.* 遗传特征　　　　　　　　　　figure *v.* 认证，认为

◆ THE MYSTERY TWIN

"I know," said Mrs Alto "Why don't we take the responses over to Mrs Jean's house? She's a genetic counselor, and spends her whole day researching and talking to parents about the *traits* they pass on to their children."

So they gathered all their responses and brought them to their next-door neighbor, Mrs Jean, and asked her for help.

The *Selection*

Mrs. Jean carefully read the interview questions and then *scanned* the responses. "First of all," she began, "let's talk about each of your questions. Your first question is about hair, and it's true that hair color and type is something passed down through your genes."

"有了，"奥托夫人说："我们为什么不把他们带去吉恩夫人家呢？她是一个遗传学顾问，整日做研究，并告诉家长们他们遗传给了孩子哪些特征。"

接下来，他们将所有的应征者聚集到了邻居吉恩夫人家，以寻求帮忙。

选择

吉恩夫人仔细阅读了面试的问题并审视了每一位应征者。"首先，"她说道，"我们先谈谈你们的每一个问题。第一个问题关于头发，头发的颜色和风格的确能通过基因遗传。"

---

trait *n* 特征，特点
scan *v.* 浏览；细看

selection *n.* 选择

GROWING PAINS I

"Jeans, like blue jeans?" asked Heather.

"Actually, I meant genes, spelled G-E-N-E-S, which are *units* of heredity that transfer traits like hair and eye color from one generation to the next," Mrs. Jean explained.

"Human genes are found in pairs, and you get one from your mother and one from your father. Genes can either be *dominant* or *recessive*, which means that a dominant gene will always *override* a recessive gene. For example, with hair, the genes for brown hair and curly hair are dominant, while the genes for blond hair and straight hair are recessive."

"So that means my twin has to have curly brown hair, like I do," said Heather.

"牛仔裤，是蓝色的牛仔裤？"（译者注：英语里"基因genes"与"牛仔裤jeans"发音相同）希瑟问道。

"我实际上说的是基因，G-E-N-E-S这样拼写，是遗传的组成单位，如头发或眼睛颜色等特征，会被一代代传下去。"吉恩夫人解释说。

"人类的基因是成对出现的，你从母亲那里得到一个，从父亲那里得到另一个。基因可以呈显性或隐性，也就是说，显性基因永远都会遮住隐性基因。例如头发，棕色的卷发基因呈显性，然而金色的直发基因呈隐性。"

"那么也就是说，我的孪生同胞像我一样，有棕色的卷发。"希瑟说。

---

unit *n.* 单位；部件
recessive *adj.* 隐性的
dominant *adj.* 显性的
override *v.* 压倒；优先于

◆ THE MYSTERY TWIN

"Not necessarily. Hair is something you can change by *bleaching* blond or *straightening*. So I would say that you can't really use hair type to indicate heredity unless you know for certain that the person has not changed his or her hair in any way."

"I guess we don't know whether or not any of our finalists changed their hair," said Mrs. Alto.

"Now, about eye color; the brown-eye gene is dominant while the blue-eye gene is recessive, so eye color used to be a very good *indicator* of heredity. But nowadays, people can wear colored contact *lenses* and change the color of their eyes."

"I suppose you're right," said Heather, trying not to sound disappointed.

"不完全是。头发是你可以通过漂成金色或拉直而改变的。所以我要说，你不能用头发的样式作为遗传的根据，除非你确定那个人从来没有改变过他的头发。"

"我想我们并不知道应征者有没有改变他们的头发。"奥托夫人说。

"现在，关于眼睛颜色的问题，棕色眼睛的基因呈显性，但蓝色眼睛的基因呈隐性，所以眼睛的颜色曾经一直以来都是一个很好的遗传标志。但是现在，人们可以戴有色隐形眼镜来改变眼睛的颜色。"

"我想你说的对。"希瑟说道，她尽量不流露出此时的失望。

---

bleach *v.* 漂白；脱色
indicator *n.* 标志；指示物

straighten *v.* 把……弄直
lens *n.* 隐形眼镜

GROWING PAINS I

"And three of these other questions about liking chess, cats, and peanut butter all deal with *acquired* traits, which means they're all things you can learn to like or not like. You aren't necessarily born liking chess, cats, or peanut butter, so I'm afraid these questions will not help you find your twin."

Heather's head *hung* low, as did Mr. and Mrs. Altos'. It seemed they had asked all the wrong questions.

"Don't look so discouraged! This last question about attached earlobes may be the key," said Mrs. Jean. "The gene for attached earlobes is recessive, while the gene for unattached earlobes is dominant. In order for a recessive trait like that to appear, both of Heather's genes for earlobes must be recessive, so she knows each

---

"像喜欢象棋、猫和花生酱这三个问题，都是后天获得的特征，这意味着这些事是你可以学着喜欢或不喜欢的。你不一定是生下来就喜欢象棋、猫和花生酱，所以恐怕这三个问题也不能帮你找到你的孪生同胞。"

希瑟低下了头，奥托夫妇也是一样。似乎他们提出的问题都是无关的。

"不要泄气嘛！最后一个关于耳垂的问题可能是关键。"吉恩夫人说："无耳垂的基因呈隐性，有耳垂的基因呈显性。要想呈现隐性遗传特征，希瑟的两个跟耳垂有关的基因必须都是隐性的，所以她的父母都应携

---

acquired *adj.* 后天的；已获得的　　　　　　　　　　hang *v.* 垂落

parent carried at least one recessive earlobe gene."

Mrs. Jean *paused* for a moment and picked up the picture of Heather's parents. "Look at your birth parents—you can see they both have attached earlobes, so you know that both of their genes were also recessive. There is no way that two parents who carry only recessive genes could have children with unattached earlobes!"

Heather began thinking out loud, "Okay . . . both my parents had attached earlobes, which makes sense because I have attached earlobes, too. That means that my twin must have attached earlobes, and the only one of the finalists who does is Harry. Harry is my twin!"

带至少一个跟耳垂有关的隐性基因。"

吉恩夫人停顿了片刻，并拿起希瑟父母的照片："看看你的亲生父母——他们俩都没有耳垂，所以他们跟耳垂有关的基因都是隐性的。父母双方都只携带隐性基因是不可能生出带耳垂的孩子的！"

希瑟重新仔细地考虑，大声说："好吧……我的父母都没有耳垂，所以我也就没有耳垂。那么我的孪生同胞也一定没有耳垂，所以候选人中唯一一个没有耳垂的就是哈利。哈利就是我的孪生弟弟！"

---

pause *v.* 停顿；暂停

GROWING PAINS I

"That's right, Harry could possibly be your twin," said Mrs. Jean. "But he also may not. It may be just a *coincidence* that his birthday is the same as yours, that he came from the same adoption agency, and that you both have attached earlobes. In order to be certain that he is your twin you should both have your DNA tested. DNA carries your genetic *code*. If your DNA carries some of the same codes, then you are brother and sister."

"But... I thought my twin would be a girl," said Heather.

Mrs. Jean responded, "Only identical twins are the same gender, because identical twins have exactly the same genes. They were born from the same egg that *split* in two, but *fraternal* twins were born

---

"是的，哈利有可能跟你是双胞胎。"吉恩夫人说："但他也可能不是。他的生日跟你一样，他跟你来自同一个领养机构，你们都没有耳垂，这也可能是一种巧合。为了确定你们是双胞胎，你们应该做个DNA测试。DNA携带你们的遗传密码。如果你们的DNA携带一些相同的密码，那你们就可能是姐弟。"

"可是……我原以为我的孪生同胞会是一个女孩。"希瑟说。

吉恩夫人回答说："只有同卵双胞胎才有相同的性别，因为同卵双胞胎具有完全相同的基因。他们是从同一个卵子一分为二的，但是异卵双胞胎由两个不同的卵子而来，他们同普通的兄弟姐妹一样，只不过是在同一

---

coincidence *n.* 巧合；一致
split *v.* 分裂；分离

code *n.* 密码；代码
fraternal *adj.* 异卵双生的

◆ THE MYSTERY TWIN

from two different eggs. They're more like regular siblings, only they were born at the same time."

"So, if Harry and I get our DNA tested we can find out for sure whether or not we are twins. Let's go tell Harry!" Heather exclaimed.

The Happy *Reunion*

The Altos quickly called Harry and his family, who were *thrilled* to hear that Harry and Heather might be twins.

The next night, the Altos invited Harry and his family for dinner. Harry and Heather discovered that there were a lot of things they had in common. Both were left-handed and both laughed as they

---

时间出生罢了。"

"那么，只要我和哈利得到我们DNA测试的结果，我们就能确定我们是不是双胞胎了。我们去告诉哈利吧！"希瑟兴奋地说。

幸福的团聚

奥托一家立刻通知了哈利和他的家人，如果他们知道哈利和希瑟可能是一对双胞胎，他们一定也很激动。

第二条晚上，奥托一家邀请哈利和他的家人共进晚餐。哈利和希瑟发现他们有许多共同点。他们俩都是左撇子，并且在笑的时候都想卷舌头又卷不起来。他们都是在10个月大的时候，长出了第一颗牙齿。并且，他们

---

reunion n. 重聚；团聚   thrilled adj. 非常兴奋的；极为激动的

GROWING PAINS I

tried in vain to *roll* their tongues. Both got their first tooth at ten-months-old and named their first pet Socks. After talking things over, both families agreed to get the children's DNA tested. However, they all agreed that they had enjoyed each others company so much that they *anticipated* spending a lot of time together in the future, even if Harry wasn't Heather's twin.

都给他们的第一只宠物起名为萨克斯。谈话结束后，双方家庭都同意让孩子做DNA测试。然而，即使哈利和希瑟不是双胞胎，他们也都同意，今后让孩子们有更多时间相处，因为他们俩在一起很开心。

---

roll v. 使……卷起　　　　　　　　　　anticipate v. 期望；预见

13

Tessa's Family Day

Concert Makes Waves

Bree *squealed* excitedly as Tessa *bounced* around the living room *grinning* like a fool and waving the newspaper up and down. Blake Baker, their favorite hip-hop rock icon, would be performing at the local *megamall* in two weeks. "Amazing! Terrific! Fantastic! I can't believe it, our first rock concert!" Bree exclaimed.

"I know. My mom will totally freak. She doesn't like Blake Baker

---

泰莎的家庭日

演唱会的风波

布瑞兴奋地尖叫着，泰莎也在客厅里像个傻瓜一样地欢呼雀跃着，还挥舞着报纸。两周后，她们最喜欢的嘻哈摇滚偶像——布莱克·贝克，将在当地购物中心举行演唱会。布瑞兴奋地叫着："真不可思议！太棒了！太棒了！我简直不敢相信，这可是我们观看的第一场摇滚演唱会啊！"

"我知道。但是我妈妈会彻底疯掉的。她不喜欢布莱克·贝克，因为

---

squeal v. （尤指小孩）长而尖的叫声
grin v. 露齿而笑

bounce v. 跳跃
megamall n. 购物中心

GROWING PAINS I

because of that unfortunate incident with the *paparazzi*, but since she can't find anything to disapprove of in his *lyrics*, she can't object to me listening to him," Tessa explained defiantly. "She can't object to you listening to him," said Bree, "but she can object to you attending the concert, even if it is free."

"Oh, I hope she doesn't want to invite herself to make sure we 'behave'," Tessa *snorted*, imitating her mom's voice. "How embarrassing would that be?"

"Your mom is really wonderful," Bree insisted quietly but *sternly* after Tessa brought up her mother. The two hadn't been communicating well lately and Bree was concerned about her friend.

"She has to let me go," Tessa practically pleaded. "It's on a

---

她不喜欢他被狗仔队拍到的那些糗事，但是既然她找不出布莱克的歌词有不好的地方，她就不能反对我听他的歌，"泰莎挑衅地解释说。"她是不能反对你听他的歌，但是她反对你去参加他的音乐会啊，即使是免费的也不行，"布瑞说道。

"哦！我希望她不要自作主张地来干涉我们的'行动'，"泰莎轻哼着模仿着她妈妈的声音，"那该多没面子啊？"

"你妈妈是很不错的人。"在泰莎提到她妈妈时，布瑞低声但严厉地说道。她们两个最近交流得不太顺畅，布瑞有点担心她的朋友。

"她必须得让我去，"泰莎其实已经开始恳求起来。"那天正好是星

---

paparazzo *n.* 专门追踪报道名人的摄影师；狗仔队　　lyric *n.* 歌词
snort *v.* 哼鼻子　　sternly *adv.* 严厉地

◆ TESSA'S FAMILY DAY

Saturday, which is family day, but she allowed Trevor to attend that *recognition* dinner at the statehouse on a Saturday when his *wrestling* team won the state championships. It's the same idea," Tessa declared.

"Trevor *earned* that dinner. You didn't earn a trip to a concert in the mall," Bree reminded her.

Tessa looked at her friend, whose habit of being almost too honest really *irritated* her right now.

"Oh, well then, I guess I should go ask my wonderful mother about the concert," Tessa retorted. "It's two weeks away, she can't say no with so much advance notice."

期六，我们家庭日的那天。但是她却让特雷弗去参加了在州议会大厦举行的庆祝宴会，就因为周六他们的摔跤队获得了州冠军。我也想去参加演唱会，"泰莎认真地说道。

"特雷弗去晚宴是名正言顺，你为了去看演唱会可是没什么理由。"布瑞提醒着泰莎。

泰莎看着她的朋友，布瑞几乎太过诚实的习惯真是一下子惹恼了她。

"哦，那么，我想我应该去问问我那个'好'妈妈，我可不可以去看演唱会，"泰莎反驳道，"还有两周的时间呢，这么早就向她请示，她没理由不让我去。"

---

recognition *n.* 表彰；赞赏
earn *v.* 获得

wrestling *n.* 摔跤
irritate *v.* 激怒；惹恼

GROWING PAINS I

Bree shook her head back and forth and watched Tessa bound out the front door and across the street to her own house.

Family Day Runs *Aground*

Tessa crept through the front door so she could *gauge* her mother's mood before approaching her about the concert. Lately Mom had been on Misery Island. Tessa surprisingly discovered her mother smiling and humming as she prepared dinner.

Before she could think about what to say, the words just poured out of Tessa's mouth like water *gushing* over a waterfall.

"Mom, guess who's going to give a concert at the megamall in

布瑞一边摇着头,一边看着泰莎跳到门前,穿过大街回自己的房间去了。

家庭日的搁浅

泰莎蹑手蹑脚地穿过前门,想看看妈妈心情怎么样,再来问她演唱会的事。因为这段日子,妈妈情绪非常低落。可泰莎意外地发现,妈妈正一边准备着晚餐,一边面带微笑的哼着歌曲呢!

泰莎还没有想好该怎么开口时,话便从嘴里一涌而出,就像是滔滔的水从瀑布上倾泻而下似的。

"妈妈,你猜猜,两周后谁将会在巨型购物中心举行演唱会?是布

---

aground *adv.* 搁浅
gush *v.* 突然大量涌出

gauge *v.* 判定,判断(尤指人的感情或态度)

◆ TESSA'S FAMILY DAY

two weeks? It's Blake Baker! Can you believe it? My idol is going to be here, in our little town, giving a free, *live* performance. It's on a Saturday, but not for two weeks. You just have to let me go with Bree, you just have to."

Tessa's mother peered carefully at her daughter.

"Tessa, I've already volunteered all of us to help on Saturday with the local food bank's food drive. You and Trevor are *slated* for *sorting* duty to keep the canned foods and the boxes of dried goods separate. Your dad and I will be organizing the volunteers and checking on the way the food crates are loaded into the truck for delivery to the *donation* center."

Tessa's heart dropped in her chest. Not only would she miss the

---

莱克·贝克！太令人难以置信了！我的偶像要来到这里啊，就是当地的小镇，举行一场免费的现场演唱会。演唱会在周六那天，而且就只有那一个周六有。你一定得让我和布瑞去。一定要让我去。"

泰莎的妈妈认真地盯着她的女儿。

"泰莎！我已经给全家人报名在周六去我们这的救济食品发放中心的募捐活动中义务帮忙。而你和特雷弗已经被安排去整理罐装食物，还有给装箱的干货分类。我和你爸爸将要组织志愿者，还得检查食物板条箱装车。然后卡车会把食物送到募捐中心。"

泰莎垂头丧气，不仅是因为将要错过这个演唱会，还因为她将要被迫

---

live *adj.* 现场表演的
sort *v.* 把……分类整理

slate *v.* 安排；规划
donation *n.* 捐赠

GROWING PAINS I

concert, but she would also be forced into *manual* labor.

"That's so unfair, Mom," Tessa complained. "You never consider how I feel when you volunteer me for things. Who wants to sort food all day long? I don't. I won't. You can't make me!"

Tessa's mother let the words hang between them for a moment.

"Tessa, I know how you feel..."

"No, you don't!" Tessa shouted.

"Please do not raise your voice at me, Tessa. The food bank people *rely* on us to provide help. They can't supply the necessary services people require without support from volunteers. Besides, you know how important family day is. We discussed the *principles*

去干体力活。

"妈妈，你那样做不公平！"泰莎抱怨着，"在你让我去做志愿者的时候，你从来都不顾及我的感受！谁愿意一整天都在那整理食物啊？我不想，我也不愿意。你不能强迫我那样做！"

泰莎的妈妈被这些话惊住了，一时竟不知道该说些什么。

"泰莎，我明白你的感受……"

"不！你不明白！"泰莎吼着。

"泰莎！请不要对我大吼大叫。救济食品发放中心的人们需要我们的帮助。没有志愿者的支持和帮助，他们就无法提供人们所需要的服务。而

---

manual *adj.* 手工的；体力的
principle *n.* 准则
rely *v.* 依赖

◆ TESSA'S FAMILY DAY

that we believe family day represents when we started setting aside special time to be together. We all agreed that family time takes *priority* over everything else. You'll present yourself at that food drive young lady, end of story."

"Fine," Tessa stated *curtly*. "I'm going to my room to do homework."

Tessa moved like *greased* lightning. She couldn't bolt out of the kitchen quickly enough. Tessa attempted to *shrug* off the tears that were about to rain down, but once her bedroom door closed, she couldn't prevent them from pouring down her cheeks.

且，你知道家庭日的重要性吗？我们讨论过家庭日所代表的准则，所以全家人才留出特定的时间一起度过。我们都一致认为，家人在一起的时间比任何事情都重要。所以，小姐，粮食发放活动那天你必须到场，就这么定了。"

"好吧！"泰莎草草地答应着，"我要回房间做作业去了！"

泰莎的脚步如同抹了油的闪电，但她离开厨房的速度还是不够快。泰莎努力地使眼泪不要像雨滴那样落下来。但当房间门关上的瞬间，她再也抑制不住了，泪水夺眶而出，滑过脸颊……

---

priority n. 优先考虑
grease v. 给……加润滑油
curtly adv. 简短而无礼地
shrug v. 甩开；摆脱

GROWING PAINS I

On the following day at school, Tessa explained to Bree the argument that had *occurred* with her mother. Bree tried to *console* her friend, but she also reminded Tessa of the importance of sticking with commitments, which *prompted* Tessa to accuse Bree of defending her mother and effectively ended the conversation. Bree decided to give Tessa some breathing room to sort things out for herself, which meant for the rest of the week, the girls barely spoke.

Stewing on the Sandbar

On Friday when Tessa arrived home from school, feeling absolutely terrible about how she'd exploded at Bree again when her friend asked how she was feeling, she found her mother crying in the

---

第二天上学时，泰莎向布瑞提起她和妈妈之间的争吵。布瑞试着去安慰她的朋友，同时也提醒泰莎，兑现自己做出的承诺是很重要的。这使泰莎认为布瑞在帮她妈妈说话，她们的对话也就到此结束了。布瑞决定给泰莎一些空间，让她自己整理一下思绪。这意味着，这两个女孩子这个星期几乎是不会再讲话了。

沙堤上的思考

泰莎星期五放学回到家里，感觉简直糟糕透顶。因为当布瑞问她心情怎么样的时候，她居然又一次向布瑞发火了。泰莎看见妈妈在厨房里哭泣。她心想，好了吧，这下真正地明白我的感受了。泰莎趁她妈妈还不知

---

occur *v.* 发生；出现
prompt *v.* 引起；激起
console *v.* 安慰；慰藉
stew *v.* 思考；担忧

◆ TESSA'S FAMILY DAY

kitchen. Good, Tessa thought, now, she really does know how I feel. Tessa hurried upstairs to her room before her mother could realize she was home.

When Tessa awoke Saturday morning, her thoughts wandered to why her mother was crying. Could she be as upset as I am about our fights? I *bet* it's work that is bothering her and not our fights—work's more important anyway.

Tessa *switched* her thoughts to today's family activity—a water park—an experience she'd *anticipated* since her dad first read the newspaper article about the park's opening. Tessa's dad was the coach for the local high school's swim team, who called him "Coach

---

道她已经回家，匆忙地上楼回到了房间。

　　泰莎星期六早上醒来的时候，还一直在想，不知妈妈为什么哭。妈妈是因为我们之间的争吵而心烦吗？我敢打赌，一定是工作的事情让她恼怒的，而不会是我们的争吵——不管怎样，对于她来说工作才是重要的。

　　接下来，泰莎对于今天的家庭活动的想法有所转变了——一个水上乐园——自从她的爸爸在报纸上第一次看到一篇关于水上乐园开放的文章后，泰莎就一直期望来这了。泰莎的爸爸是当地高中游泳队的教练，被人们以神话中海神的名字命名为"海神教练"，而泰莎的妈妈，在大学时也

---

bet　*v.*　打赌；敢断定　　　　　　　　　switch　*v.*　转变；改变
anticipate　*v.*　期望；盼望

Neptune" after the *mythical* god of the seas; and Tessa's mom had swum competitively in college.

Tessa's parents always said she and Trevor came naturally by their love of water recreation— and Tessa did love the *substance* from which all life springs, as her mother would say. Tessa's mom often shared a story with anyone who would listen about how each of her children seemed to swim like *backstroking* Olympians even in the *womb*.

Tessa decided to try to forget about the events of the past week and concentrate on enjoying a day of water slides, inflatable beach toys, and machine-generated waves.

Struggling Loose with the Tide

After a stiff picnic lunch with her family later in the afternoon,

---

曾是一个游泳健将。

泰莎的父母总是说，泰莎和特雷弗与生俱来便带着他们对于水中娱乐项目的热爱——泰莎也正如她妈妈说的那样，喜欢这种充盈着生命活力的物质。泰莎的妈妈经常对别人讲，她的孩子们在她肚子里的时候，就像奥运会选手一样会仰泳了。

而泰莎决定试着忘记过去一周所发生的种种不愉快，专心地享受今天。享受着水上滑梯，充气的沙滩玩具以及机器运转激起的浪花。

风浪中的挣扎

下午，全家人的野餐气氛有点僵。泰莎想要去享受一下泳池旁的安静

---

mythical *adj.* 神话的　　　　　　　　substance *n.* 物质
backstroke *n.* 仰泳　　　　　　　　　womb *n.* 子宫；腹部；肚子

◆ TESSA'S FAMILY DAY

and then trying to enjoy the time in a quiet corner of the wave pool, Tessa *braced* herself as she saw her mother swimming toward her.

"Tessa, we should talk," her mother stated softly.

"Okay," agreed Tessa, causing *ripples* in the water as she crossed her arms over her chest.

"Do you remember when you were a little girl and I was home all the time?"

"Sure," answered Tessa, not sure where this conversation was headed.

"Well, since I went back to work, things have been very different between you and me."

"You went back to work ages ago," Tessa reminded her.

角落。她正撑着身体，就看见妈妈向自己游来。

"泰莎，我想我们应该好好谈谈，"泰莎的妈妈温和地说。

"好的，"泰莎呼应着。她把双手交叉放在胸前，使得水池中激起层层波浪。

"你还记着你小时候，我一直在家的日子吗？"

"当然记得了，"泰莎答道，不明白妈妈这次想谈些什么。

"但是，自从我重新开始工作后，我们之间的关系就变得糟糕了。"

"你很多年前就重新开始工作了，"泰莎提醒道。

---

brace v. 支撑　　　　　　　　　　　　ripple n. 微波；涟漪

GROWING PAINS I

"That's true. But recently I've realized how much I miss staying home with you and your brother and volunteering at your schools. It's really become clear to me how much you're growing up without me around. I'm angry with myself for what I'm missing—how much I miss you."

Tessa's *stomach* dropped like a *lead balloon*, and her arms *followed suit*. Immediately she wished she could take back every *horrid* thought her mind created about her mother, especially over the past week.

"I miss you, too. In fact, Mom, I miss you so much it makes me angry sometimes, too. We don't talk anymore—at least not like

"是的，但我最近发现，我好怀念待在家里陪伴着你和你哥哥的时光，乐此不疲地关心着你们的学习。而且，我真真切切地感觉到，在我不在你们身边的时间里，你们也成长了很多。我很气自己，对于你们，我错过了太多。我真的很想念你。"

泰莎的小腹像铅球一样沉了下去，她的手臂也不由自主地放了下来。突然间，她希望自己能够收回之前所有关于妈妈的糟糕的想法，特别是上周的那些偏见。

"我也想你，妈妈！事实上，我非常的想你，这让我有的时候很生你

stomach *n.* 肚子
follow suit 跟着做；学样

lead balloon 铅球
horrid *adj.* 讨厌的；令人不愉快的

◆ TESSA'S FAMILY DAY

we did before. We have family day, but Dad and Trevor are always around."

"I know, honey," Tessa's mother agreed, "and it won't ever be like it was before, but I think if we compromise, we can both be happier."

Tessa looked *warily* at her mother, whose face seemed to *glow* with expectation like the sun's reflection off the water.

"I *propose* that I pick you up after school Tuesday and Wednesday so we can help the food bank prepare for the donation drive and sort any food that comes in early," Tessa's mother said, smiling *tentatively*. "That will fulfill our promise to the organization and give

---

的气。我们不再谈心——至少不像以前那样亲密了。我们虽然有家庭日，但是爸爸和特雷弗却经常不在。"

"亲爱的，我知道。"泰莎的妈妈回答着，"我们回不到过去那样的日子了。但是，我想只要我们都做出些让步，我们都会比以前更加幸福的。"

泰莎羞涩地看着妈妈，妈妈的脸上散发着期盼的光彩，好像是水中反射出的阳光。

"我想在周二和周三放学后去接你。然后帮救济食品发放中心为募捐食物活动做准备——处理那些提前运到的各种食物。"泰莎的妈妈带着询问的微笑。"那样我们就可以实现对组织的承诺，也可以给我们创造一些

---

warily *adv.* 小心地；谨慎地
propose *v.* 打算

glow *v.* 发光
tentatively *adv.* 试探性地

GROWING PAINS I

us some time together. Regularly, on Tuesdays after school, you and I can bond over water *aerobics*. On Saturday, your father and Trevor will still work during the food drive, and Saturday will continue to be family day, so we'll all have dinner and play games that night."

"However, as an *olive branch* to properly start our mother-daughter bonding time, this Saturday, you and I will attend that Blake Baker concert."

"Really? Mom, that's *phenomenal*," Tessa said, practically bubbling over with excitement. "Wahoo!"

"But wait, you really want to go to the concert?"

"I want to go with you. Besides, I need to give Blake Baker a

---

相处的时间。每周二放学后,我和你可以一起做水上有氧运动。星期六,你爸爸和特雷弗仍会在募捐处帮忙。周六仍然是我们的家庭日。我们将会一起享受晚餐,晚上一起玩游戏。"

"而且,我要为珍惜我们的母女共处的宝贵时间表示一下诚意,这个周六,我陪你去参加布莱克·贝克的演唱会。"

"真的吗?妈妈,这太出乎意料啦,"泰莎兴奋得嘴都合不上,"哇噢!"

"但是,等等,你真的想去参加这个演唱会吗?"

"我想陪你一起去。而且,我需要给布莱克·贝克一个机会,给我留

---

aerobics *n.* 有氧运动　　　　　　　　olive branch 橄榄枝;和解姿态
phenomenal *adj.* 了不起的;非凡的

second chance to make a better impression on me," Mom said, smiling. "Everyone *deserves* the chance to make up for *dreadful* behavior."

Smooth Sailing Ahead

Tessa's *effervescence* quieted. "I'm sorry, Mom. I'm sorry I didn't talk to you about why I was so angry because I thought you cared more about work than you did about me."

"I'm sorry, too, Tessa. You, Trevor, your dad— my family—are the most important things in this world. We have to better communicate our feelings to each other so we don't end up hurting each other's feelings again."

Tessa thought of a great *analogy*. "Communication is to our family

---

下点好印象。"妈妈笑道,"况且,每个人都有机会来弥补自己犯下的大错啊。"

风平浪静前行

泰莎的欢腾平静了下来,说:"妈妈,对不起。因为我没有跟你说过,我如此生气是因为我感觉,相对于我,你更关心的是你的工作。"

"泰莎,我也非常抱歉。你的爸爸、特雷弗还有你,对于我来说是这个世界上最重要的。我们应该更好地沟通我们的情感,这样我们才不会再次伤害到对方。"

泰莎想到了一个非常好的比方。"沟通对于家庭,就像水对于生命的

---

deserve *v.* 得到
effervescence *n.* 兴高采烈;热情洋溢

dreadful *adj.* 糟透的
analogy *n.* 类比;比喻

as water is to life."

"Exactly," her mom said.

"I have the best plan for making things up to you, Mom. You'll be so proud of me, but it's a surprise."

"I can't wait to hear what you have planned," her mom said, knowing that whatever surprise Tessa held up her sleeve, she was *assured* they would be making a concerted effort to bond with each other.

"It'll be amazing, darling," Tessa said, *striking* her best movie star pose, "we'll do lunch."

意义一样。"

"太对了，"妈妈说。

"妈妈，我有一个绝好的计划来弥补对你的抱歉。你会为我感到骄傲的，但这是个惊喜哦。"

"我已近迫不及待地想要知道你的计划了，"妈妈说着。她知道，无论泰莎给她一个什么样的惊喜，她都确信，她们会齐心协力地把全家人团结在一起。

"亲爱的，那一定会很棒的，"泰莎说着，并摆出最当红影星的造型，"我们将会做午餐！"

---

assure v. 使确信；担保   strike v. 摆出……的姿态

Harold the Hungry Plant

One afternoon, April was doing her homework when her father brought her a present. He handed her a funny-looking plant, called a *pitcher plant*.

"This is a special plant," he told her. "It eats *insects*."

"Wow," April replied, "that's cool."

April took the plant up to her room and set it on the *windowsill*. She wanted it to get some sun. "I'll name you Harold," she said

---

哈罗德，饥饿的植物

一天下午，艾普丽尔正在做作业，爸爸给她送来一份礼物，递到她手上的是一棵看起来很滑稽的植物，叫作猪笼草。"这是一种非常特别的植物，"爸爸告诉她，"它吃昆虫。"

"噢，"艾普丽尔回答说，"太酷了。"

艾普丽尔把这棵植物拿到自己的房间里，并放在窗台上，她想让它得到一些阳光。"我要给你起个名字，叫哈罗德，"她对这棵植物说。

---

pitcher plant 猪笼草；捕虫草
windowsill *n.* 窗台；窗沿

insect *n.* 昆虫

GROWING PAINS I

to the plant.

She began to look at the little book that came with the plant. It showed pictures of flies and *spiders* being eaten by the plant. April learned that she was only supposed to feed Harold once a week.

April went downstairs and outside. She looked around the yard and found a small *anthill*. She caught some of the ants in a jar and took them to her room.

April poured the ants into the plant tank and waited. One ant *crawled* into the plant's pitcher and got stuck. It was trapped by hairs inside of the pitcher.

April thought the way Harold ate insects was really strange, but she liked him. On her way out of her room, she grabbed some *jellybeans* from a jar on her dresser.

Harold saw this and wondered what a jellybean might taste like. Flies and ants are nice, but a red jellybean would be very nice.

　　她开始阅读和植物一起拿来的小书，上面画着这种植物吃的飞虫和蜘蛛。艾普丽尔知道了这种植物每周只喂一次就可以。

　　艾普丽尔来到了楼下，到了户外，她看一下院子的周围，看到一个小蚁丘，她用一个罐子抓了一些蚂蚁，把蚂蚁带到自己的屋里。

　　艾普丽尔把蚂蚁倒到植物的槽里面，然后等在旁边。有一只蚂蚁爬到了植物的囊叶上就被卡在上面了，这是被囊叶里面的毛抓住了。

　　艾普丽尔觉得哈罗德吃昆虫的方式很特别，但她很喜欢。她走出房间时，从衣橱里选了一些豆形软糖。

　　哈罗德看到了这些，想知道豆形软糖的味道，飞虫和蚂蚁味道不错，但是红色的豆形软糖可能会更好吃。

---

spider *n.* 蜘蛛
crawl *v.* 爬行

anthill *n.* 蚁冢
jellybean *n.* 一种豆形糖果

◆ HAROLD THE HUNGRY PLANT

The next time Harold saw April bringing him some ants, he thought about the jellybeans she always ate. He wanted a red one. But when she opened the *lid*, it was just more ants. At least they were the spicy, red kind.

The next week, April brought Harold a fat, *wiggly* worm. She dropped the worm straight into his pitcher. It was a nice treat for Harold after only eating ants for the last few weeks. But he still wanted a red jellybean.

A week later, April brought Harold more insects. Harold thought about jellybeans. He thought and thought as hard as he could. Jellybeans. Jellybeans. Jellybeans. Jellybeans.

He repeated the thought over and over. April ate a couple of jellybeans before feeding Harold more insects.

后来，哈罗德看到艾普丽尔给他带来了一些蚂蚁，他想起来她常吃的豆形软糖，想要一个红色的，但当她打开盖子后，里面只有蚂蚁。至少还味道很好，而且是红色的。

一周后，艾普丽尔给哈罗德带来了一个胖胖的、扭动着的肉虫。她把肉虫丢进囊叶里面。哈罗德最近几周一直在吃蚂蚁，所以这真是款待，但他还是想吃红色的豆形软糖。

又过了一周，艾普丽尔给哈罗德带来了很多的昆虫，而哈罗德还是在想着豆形软糖，他尽最大的可能，想呀想呀想——豆形软糖呀，豆形软糖呀，豆形软糖呀，豆形软糖呀。

他一遍遍地想来想去。艾普丽尔吃过好多豆形软糖后，才再去喂给哈罗德一些昆虫。

---

lid *n.* 盖子；顶盖　　　　　　　　wiggly *adj.* 蠕动的；蜿蜒的

GROWING PAINS I

When April opened the lid to Harold's home, she only had a couple of small spiders. Harold was disappointed that she didn't feed him a red jellybean. But he was very hungry. He felt *grateful* that April fed him so well. Yet, he really wanted a jellybean.

That night, when April was going to bed, she ate a jellybean before brushing her teeth. Then she took another one—a red one—and placed it into Harold's pitcher.

Harold was so excited that his leaves began to *shake*. The jellybean was smooth and kind of hard. As it sat inside the pitcher, it became soft and sticky. The flavor began to *ooze* out. It tasted so sweet, so wonderful. He felt himself glowing with joy.

The next day April noticed that Harold looked happy. "Hi there, Harold," she said. "You sure look happy today. Did you like the

---

艾普丽尔打开哈罗德家的盖子时，她只有几只蜘蛛，哈罗德非常失望，因为艾普丽尔没有喂他红色的豆形软糖。但他非常饿，艾普丽尔喂得他很好，他是心存感激的，只是他非常想吃豆形软糖。

那天晚上，艾普丽尔已经上床睡了，她先吃了豆形软糖后刷了牙，后来她又拿了一颗，一颗红色的，放在了哈罗德的囊叶里面。

哈罗德太高兴了，它的叶子都开始颤抖起来，豆形软糖很光滑，而且比较硬，放进囊叶后，它变得软软的，而且黏黏的，味道开始飘了出来，口味很甜，太美妙了。他感到神采飞扬。

第二天，艾普丽尔看到哈罗德很高兴，"你好，哈罗德，"她说，

---

grateful *adj.* 感激的；感谢的
ooze *v.* 冒出；散发出

shake *v.* 颤动；发抖

◆ HAROLD THE HUNGRY PLANT

jellybean?"

Harold tried to smile by curling one of his leaves. He felt very happy. He really enjoyed his jellybean.

From that day on, Harold got one red jellybean each week. It was a midweek treat between regular meals. He grew bigger and stronger. Soon, he was big enough to eat *crickets* and *grasshoppers*.

April and Harold were good friends. Harold even got to go to school with her once for show-and-tell. That day he only got a cricket to eat. A couple of days later, though, he got a green jellybean. Wow, thought Harold, all the colors are tasty.

As much as Harold loved all the colors of jellybeans, red ones were still his favorites.

"你今天看起来非常高兴，你喜欢豆形软糖吗？"

哈罗德卷起叶子，想表达自己的微笑，他是太高兴了，他真的喜欢豆形软糖。

从那以后，哈罗德每周都能吃到一颗红色的豆形软糖，这是每周正常饮食以外的"周间款待"，他长大了，结实了。很快他就可以吃蟋蟀和蚱蜢了。

艾普丽尔和哈罗德成了好朋友，有一次艾普丽尔还把哈罗德带到学校，在课上给同学们做了展示。哈罗德那天只吃了一个蟋蟀，几天后，它吃了一颗绿色的豆形软糖。哇，哈罗德想，所有的颜色都很好吃。

哈罗德喜欢所有颜色的豆形软糖，但是红色还是他最喜欢的。

---

cricket *n.* 蟋蟀   grasshopper *n.* 蝗虫；蚂蚱